GARDENS
IN
BLOOM

A Colouring Book
for relaxation and rejuvenation

Cassie Haywood

ISBN: 978-0-9944431-2-0

A CIP record for this book is available from the National Library of Australia

GARDENS IN BLOOM

Gardens enable you to witness firsthand how the miracle of life happens. There is something amazing and heart-opening about observing the natural rhythms of nature. Natural environments promote calmness and well-being, therefore spending time in the garden can bring peace when your soul is restless, allowing your mood to soften. A little dose of nature certainly helps us all to recharge.

In this book you will find 50 illustrations inspired from the garden. Simply choose an illustration which appeals to you, take a few deep breaths and start colouring. There are no rules to follow, you choose the medium and colours which speak to you. These illustrations open the way for letting go and inner peace, therefore allowing relaxation and rejuvenation to become part of your everyday life.

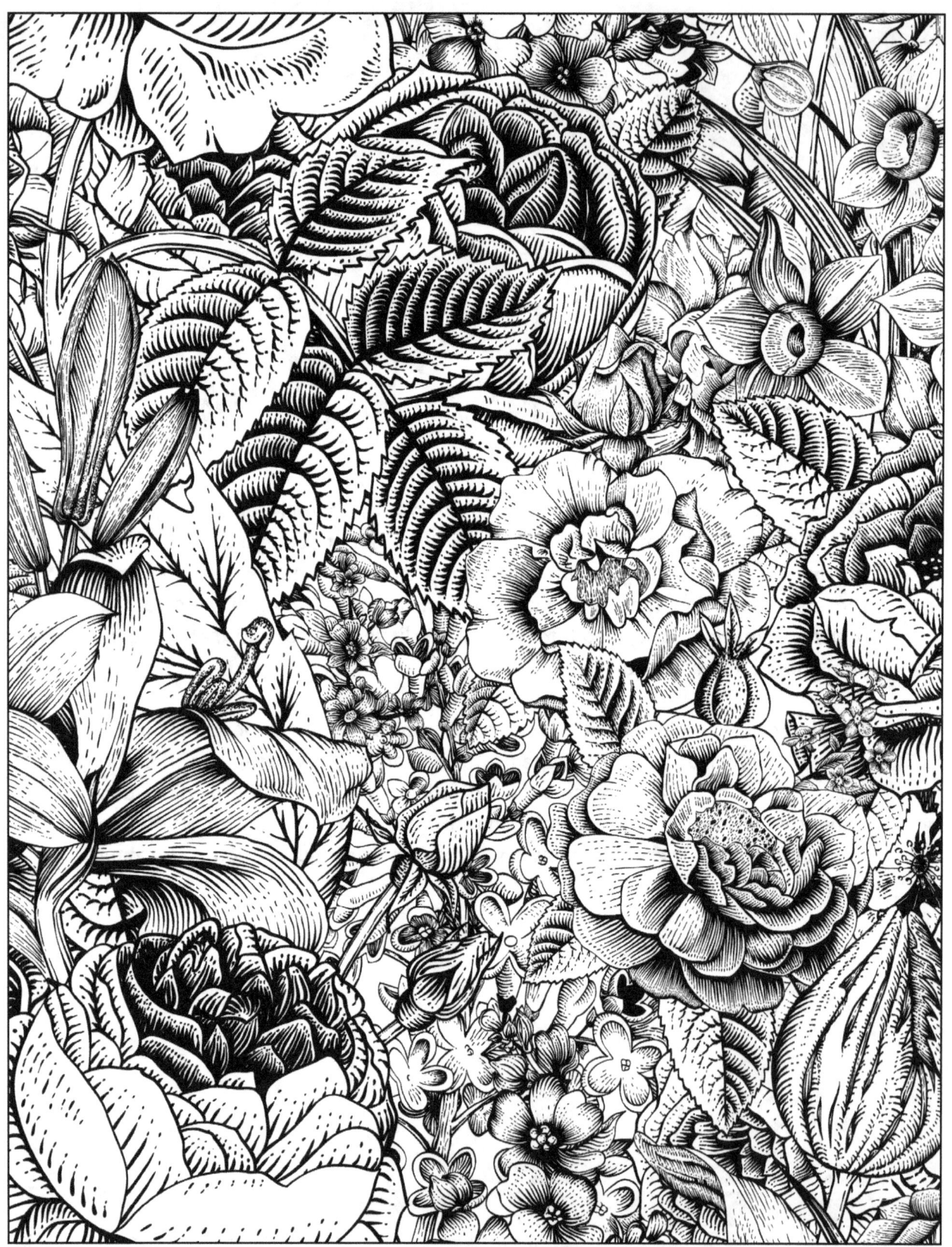

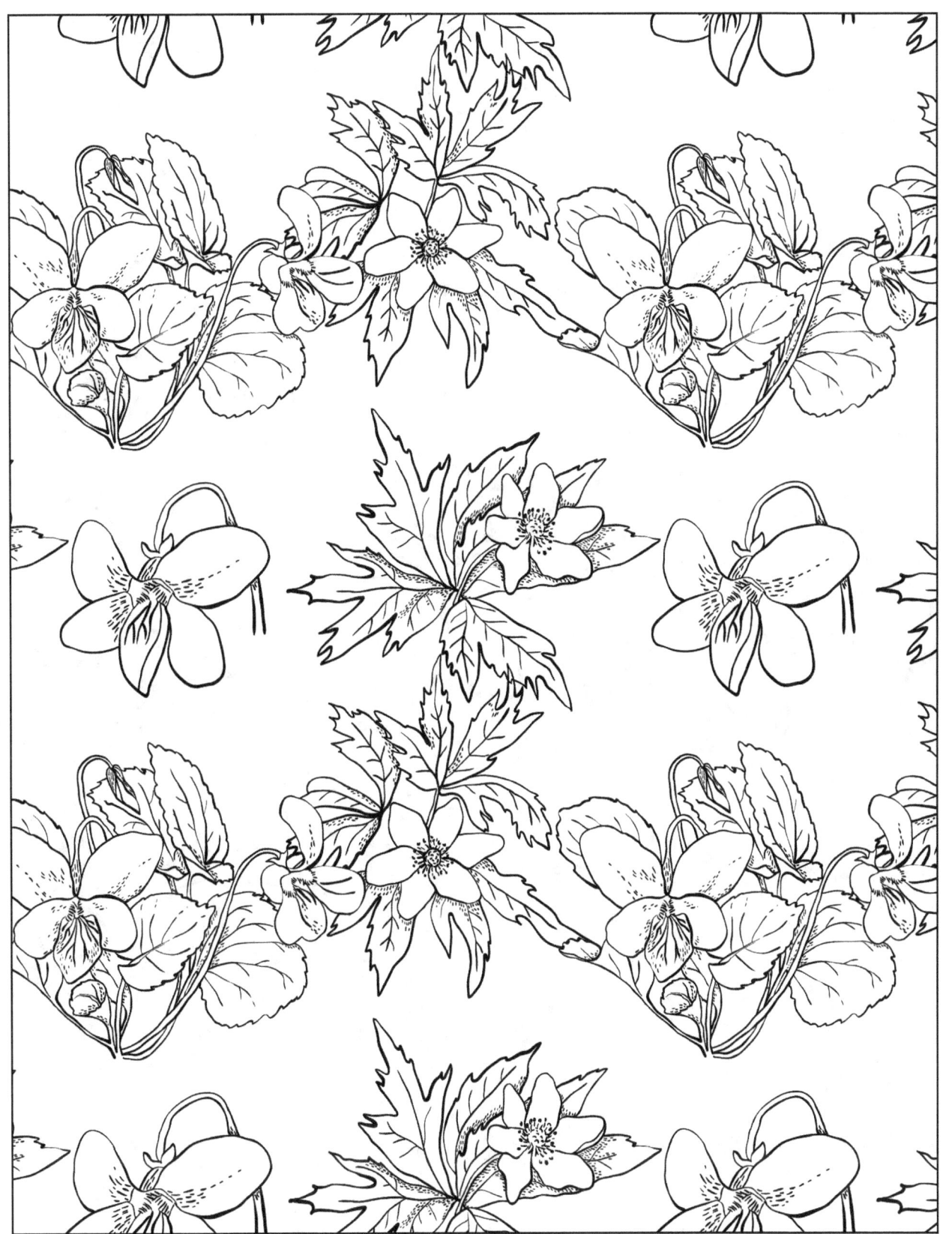

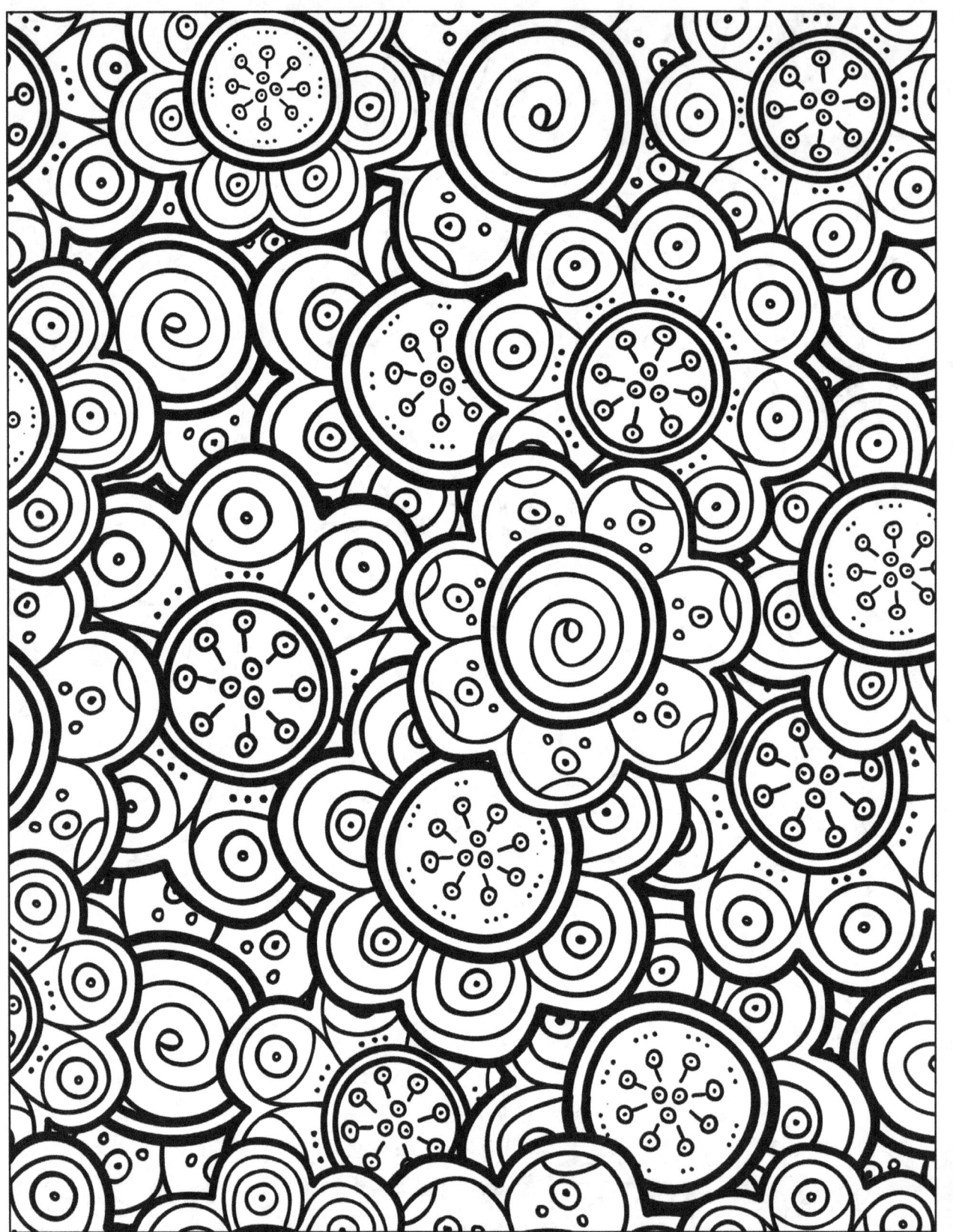

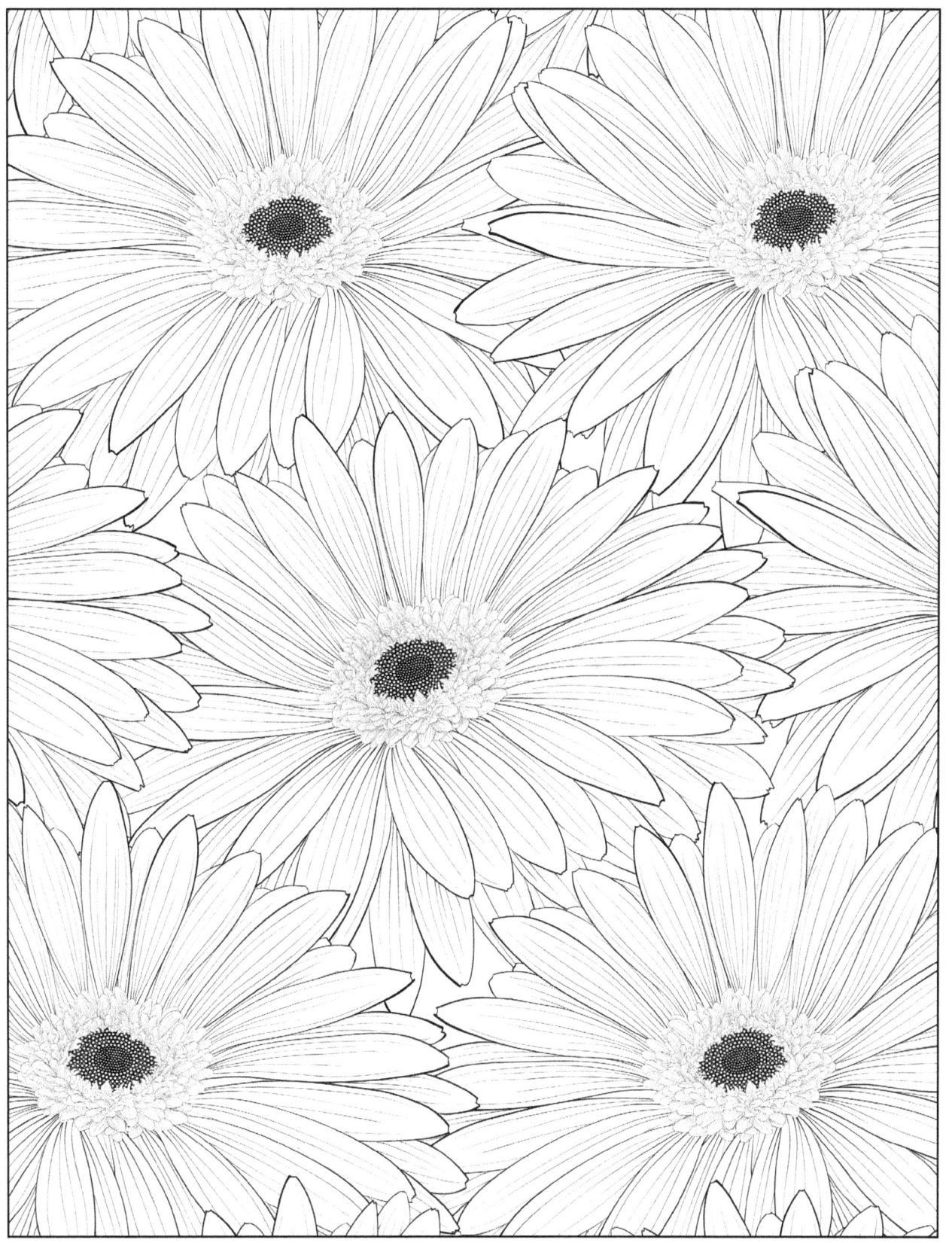

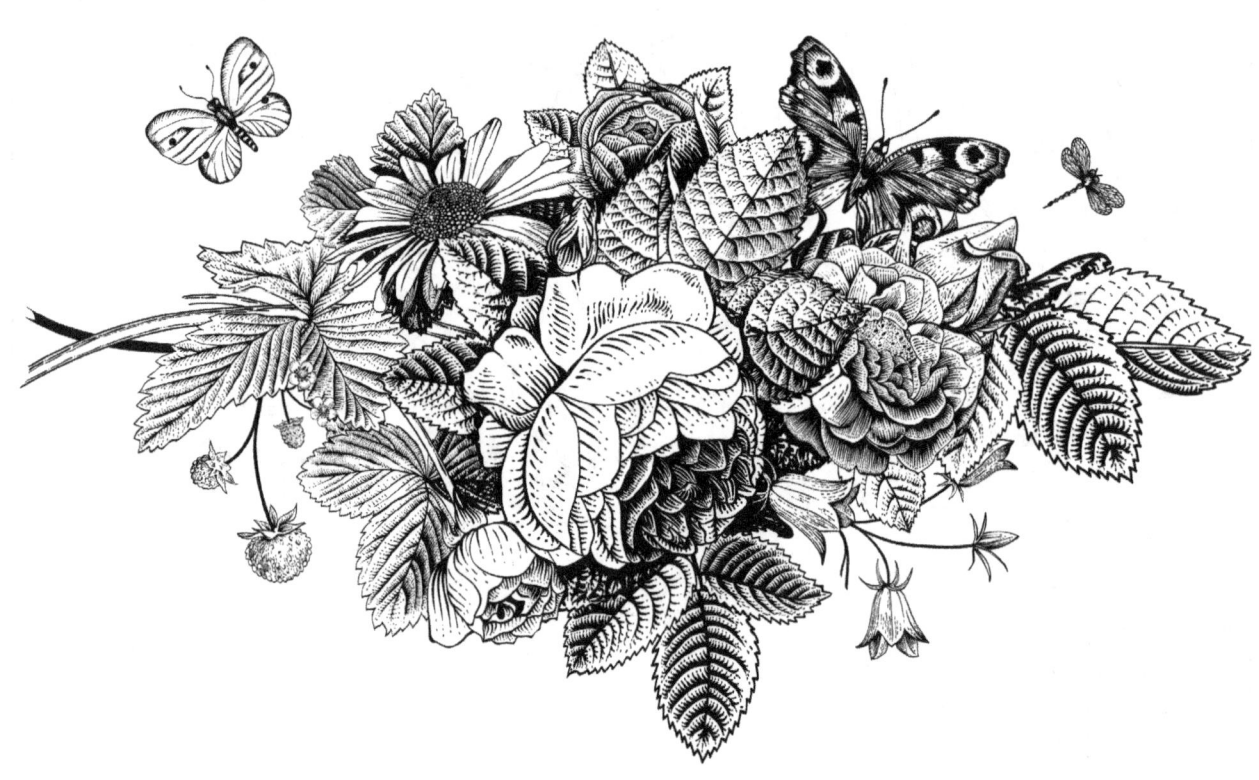

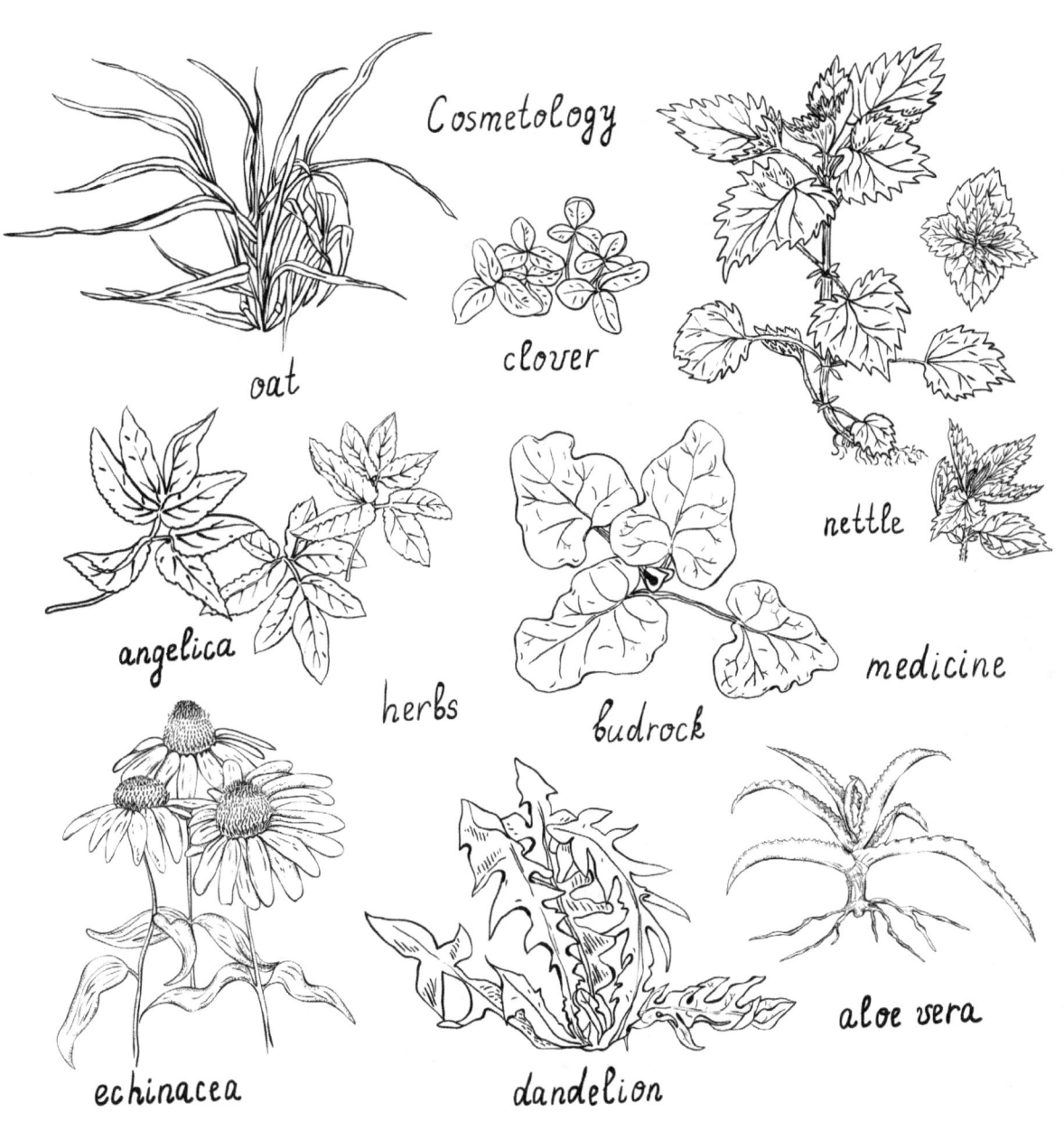

Cosmetology

oat

clover

nettle

angelica

herbs

budrock

medicine

echinacea

dandelion

aloe vera

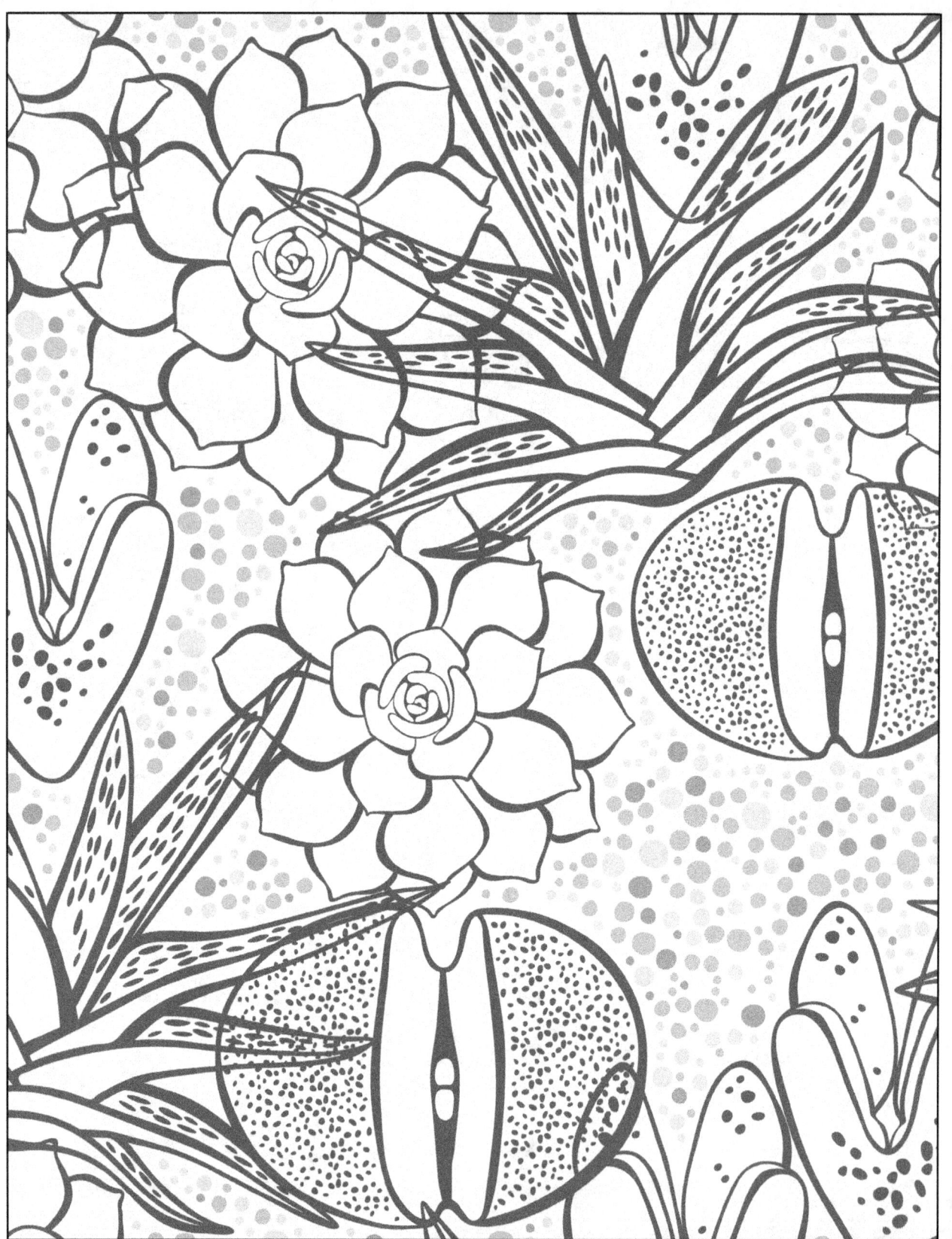

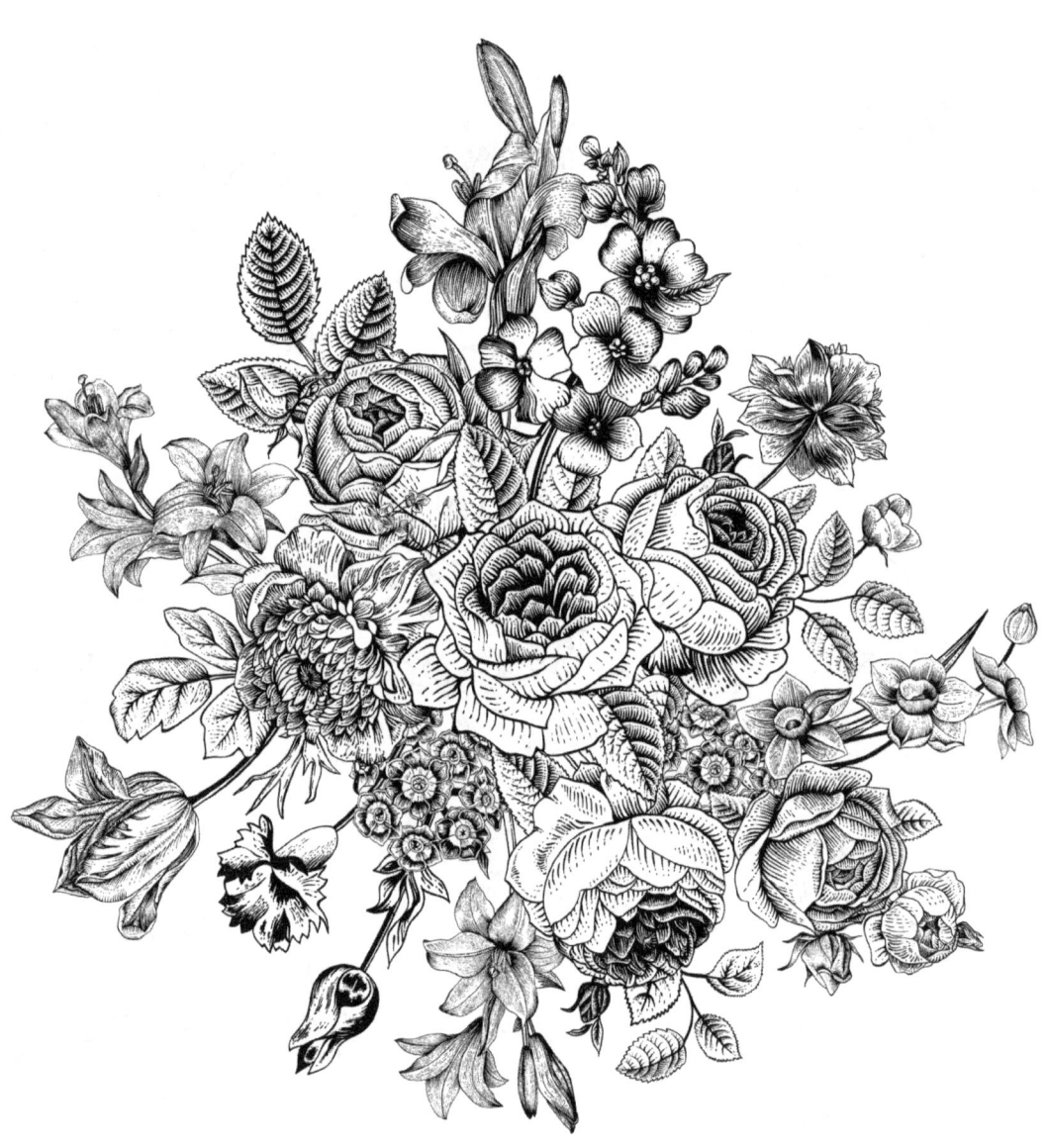

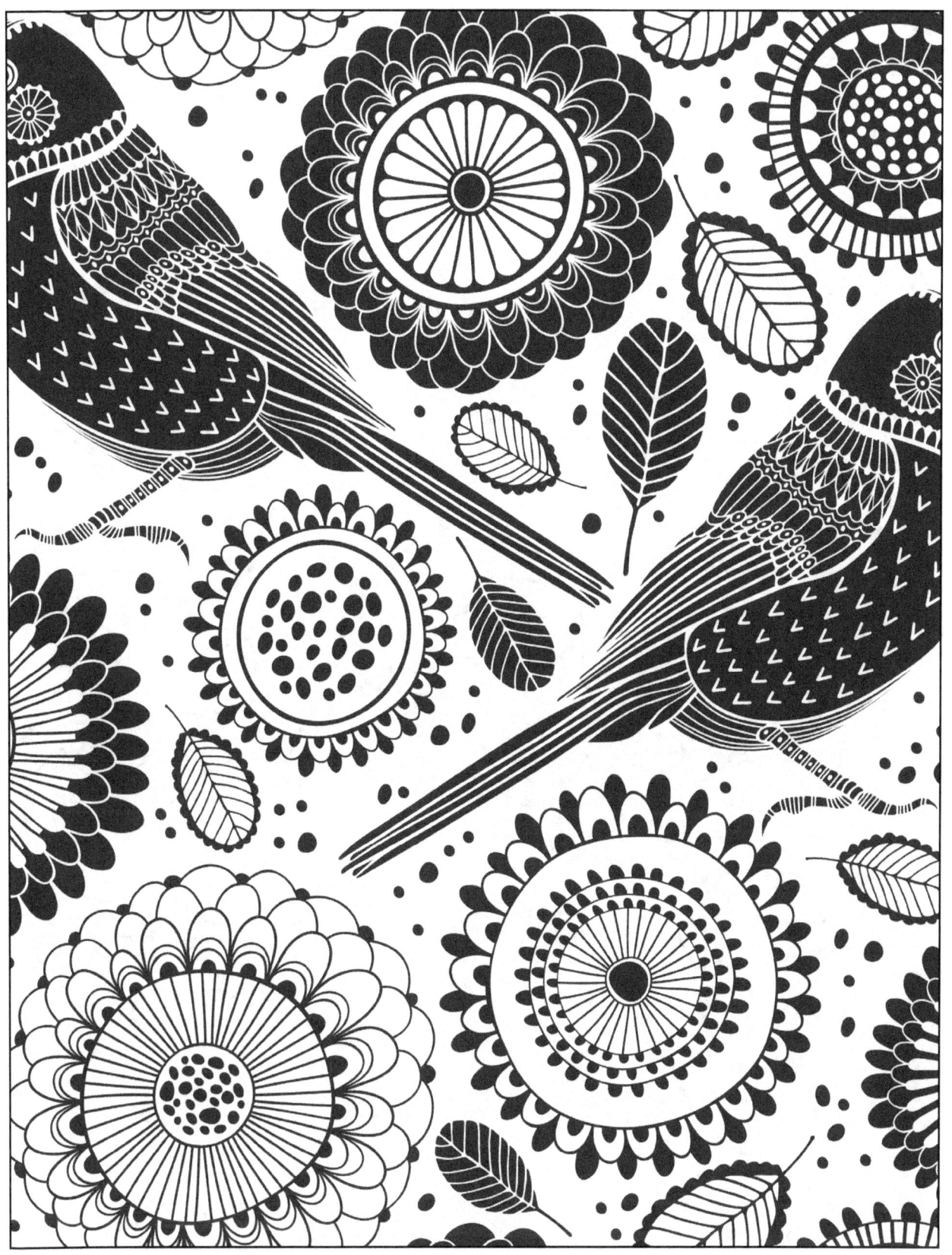

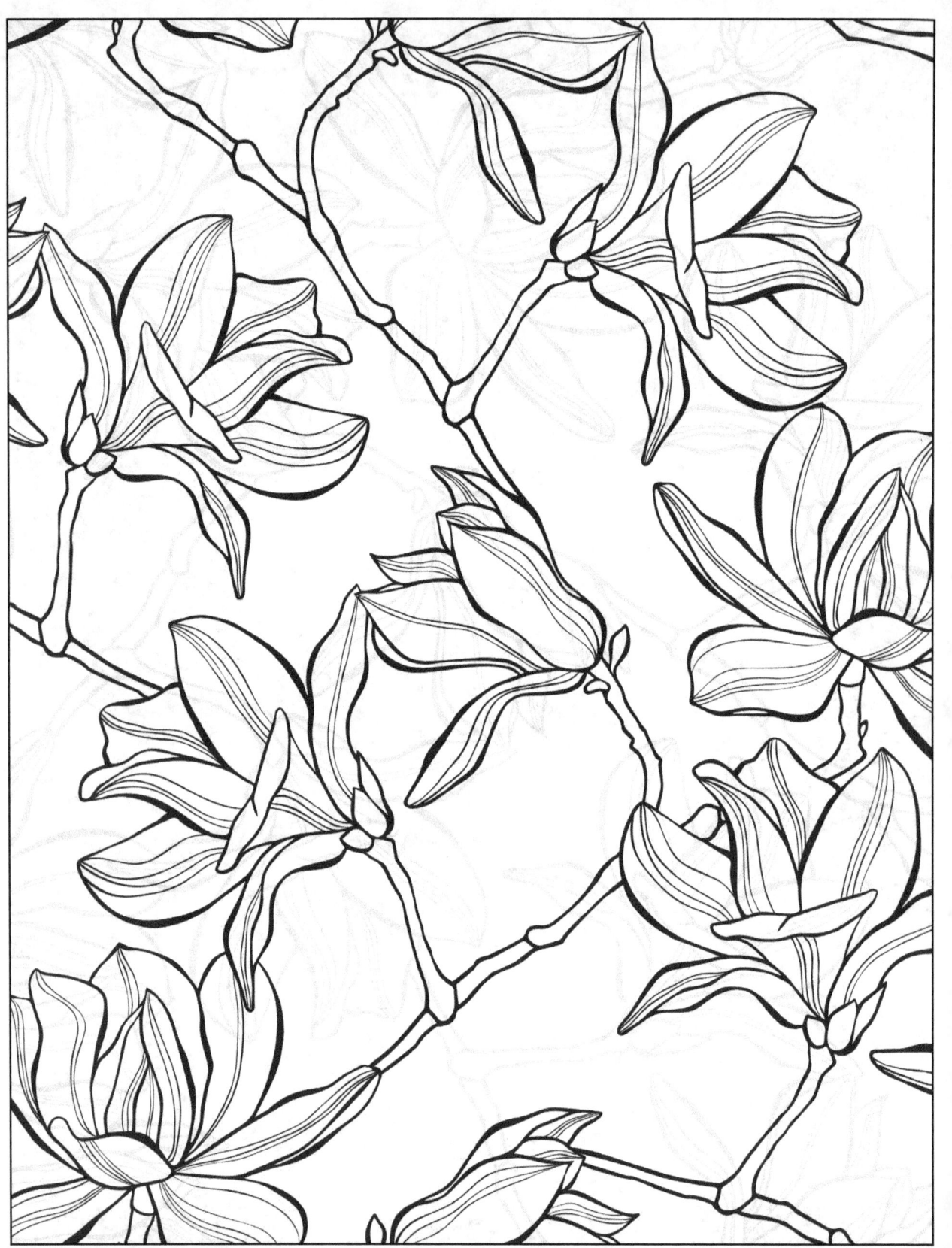

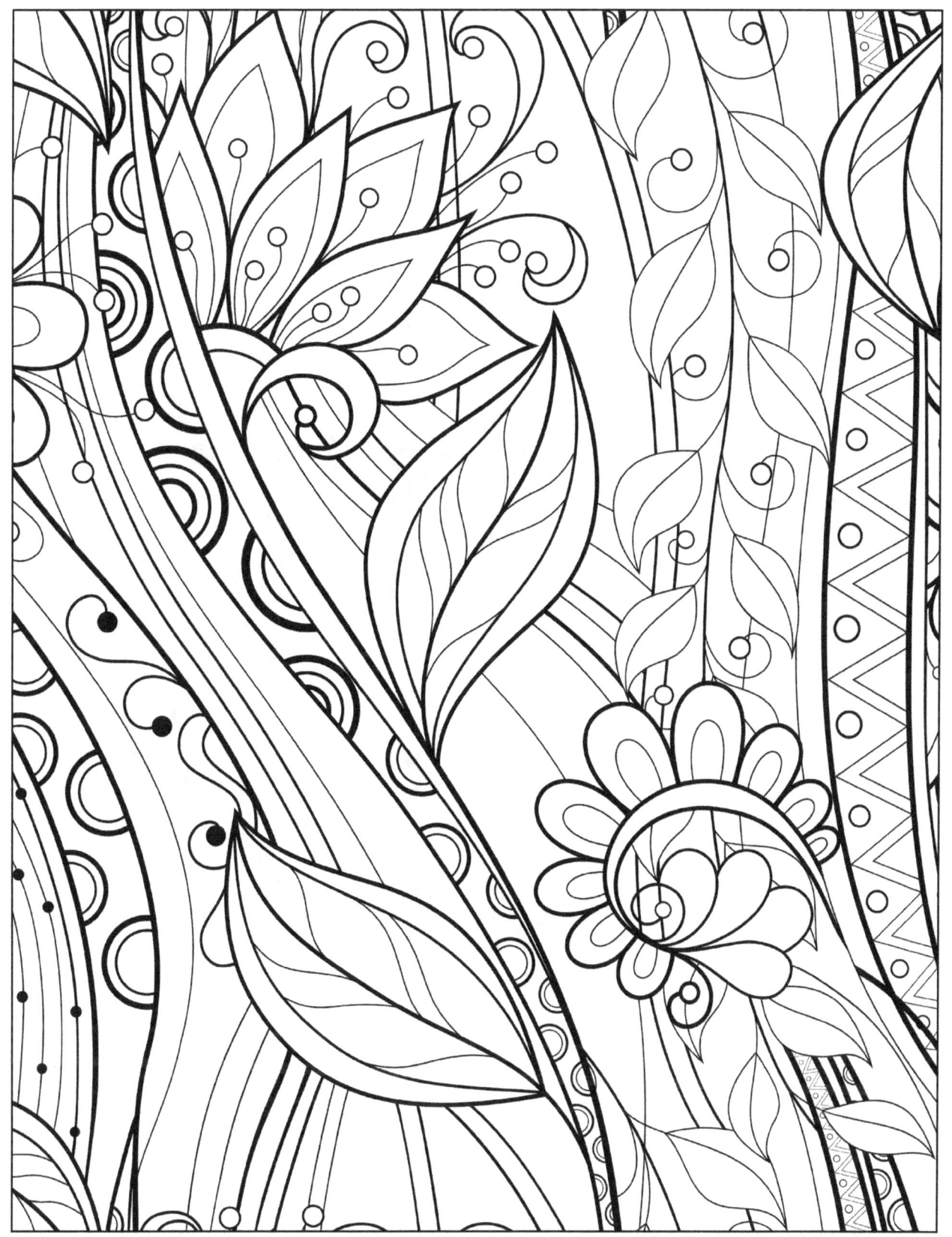

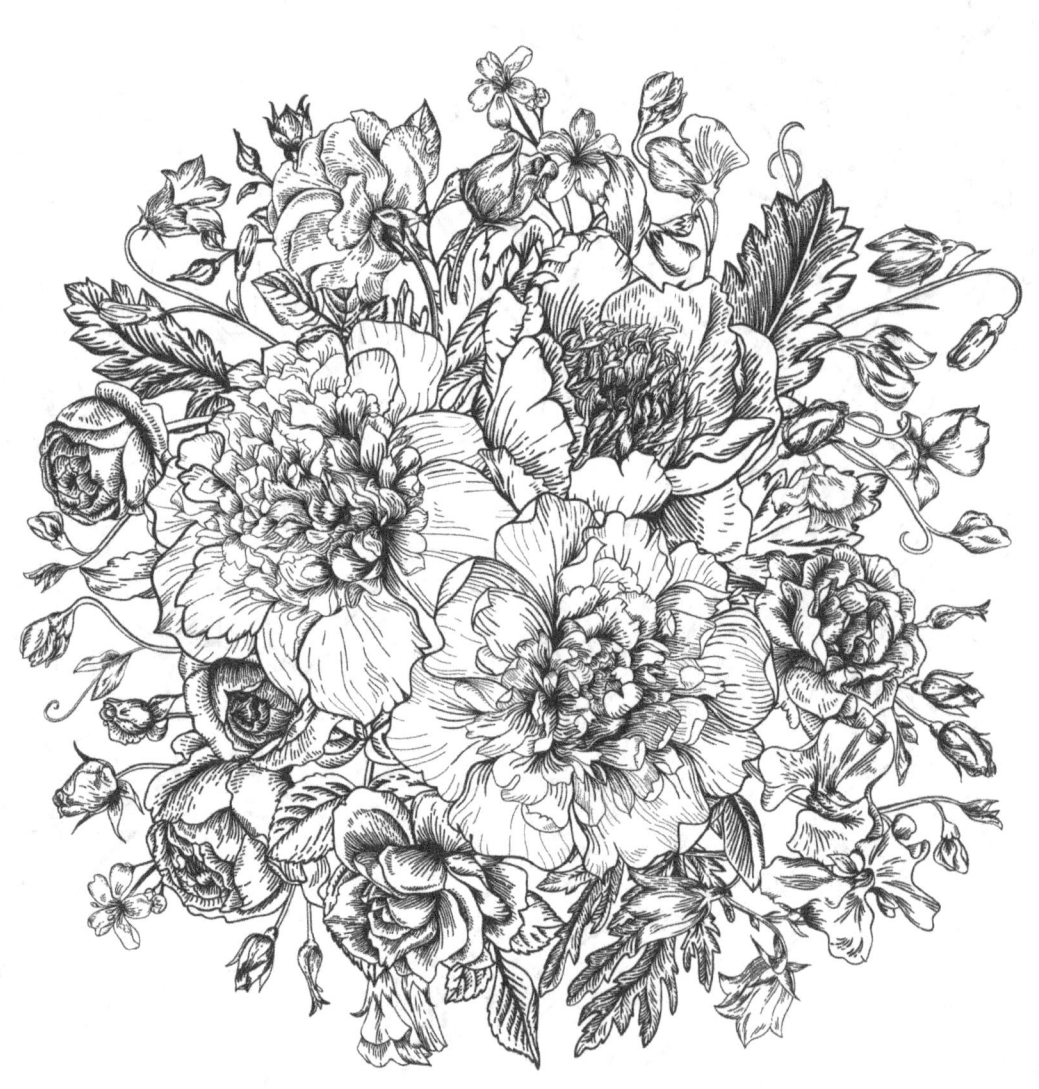

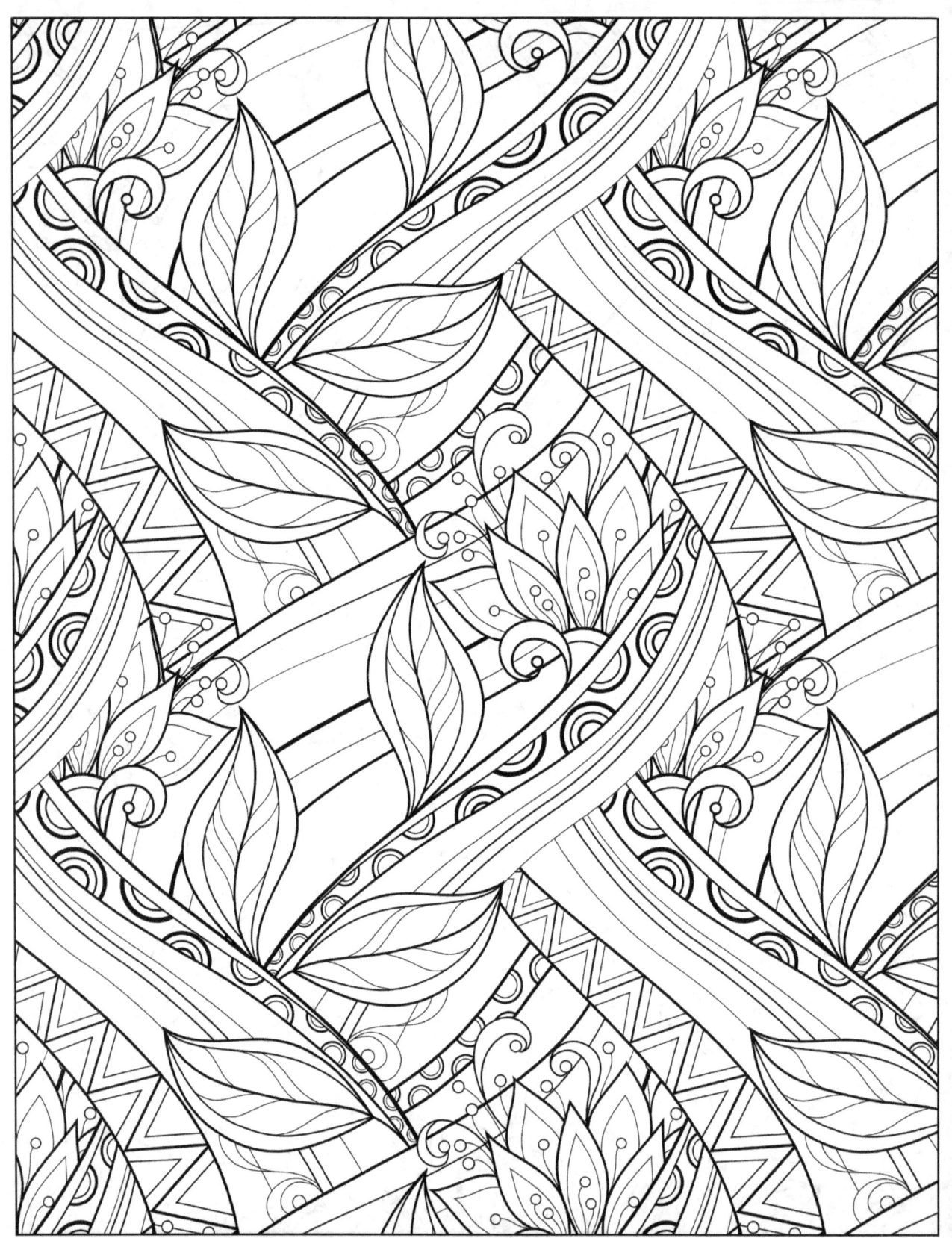

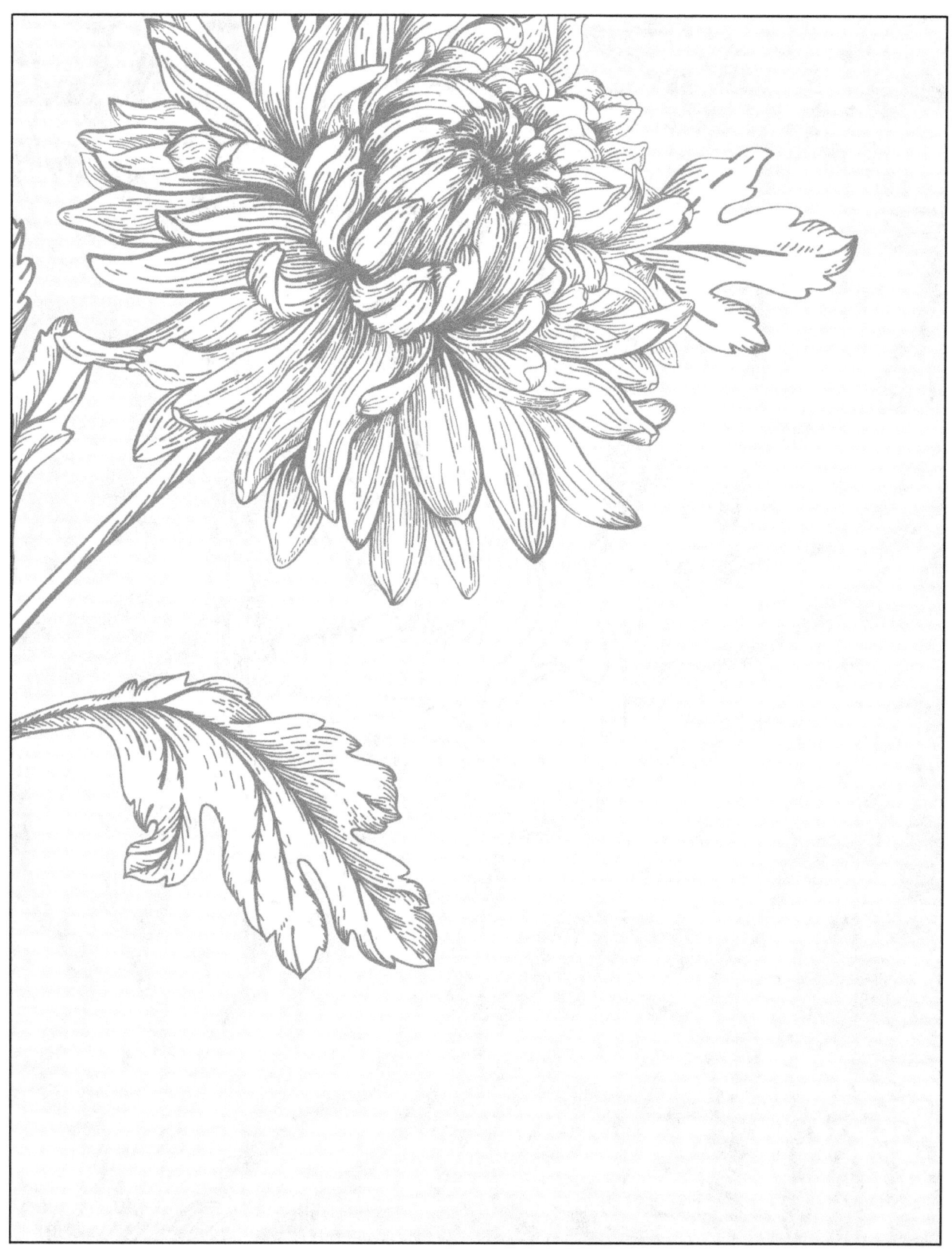

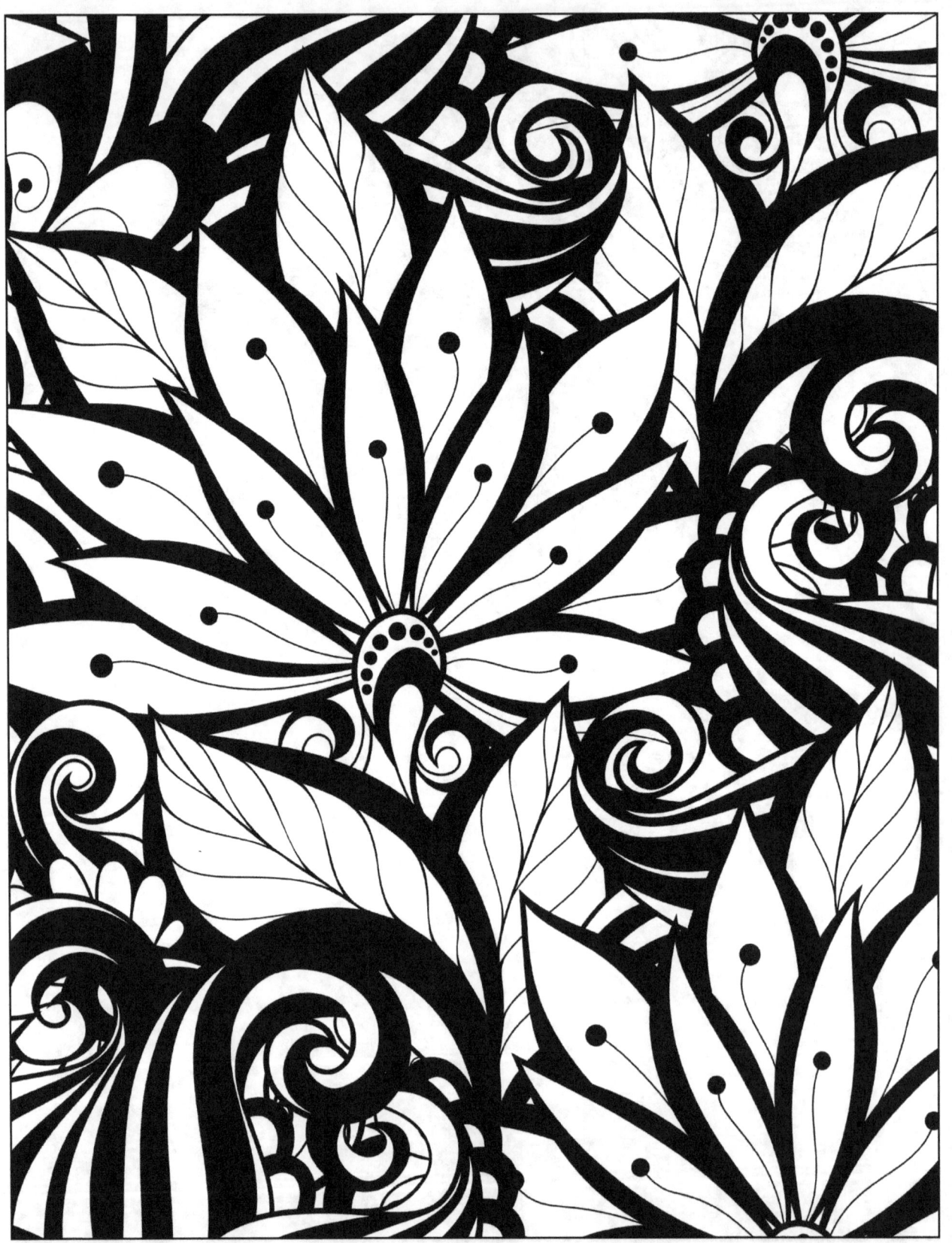

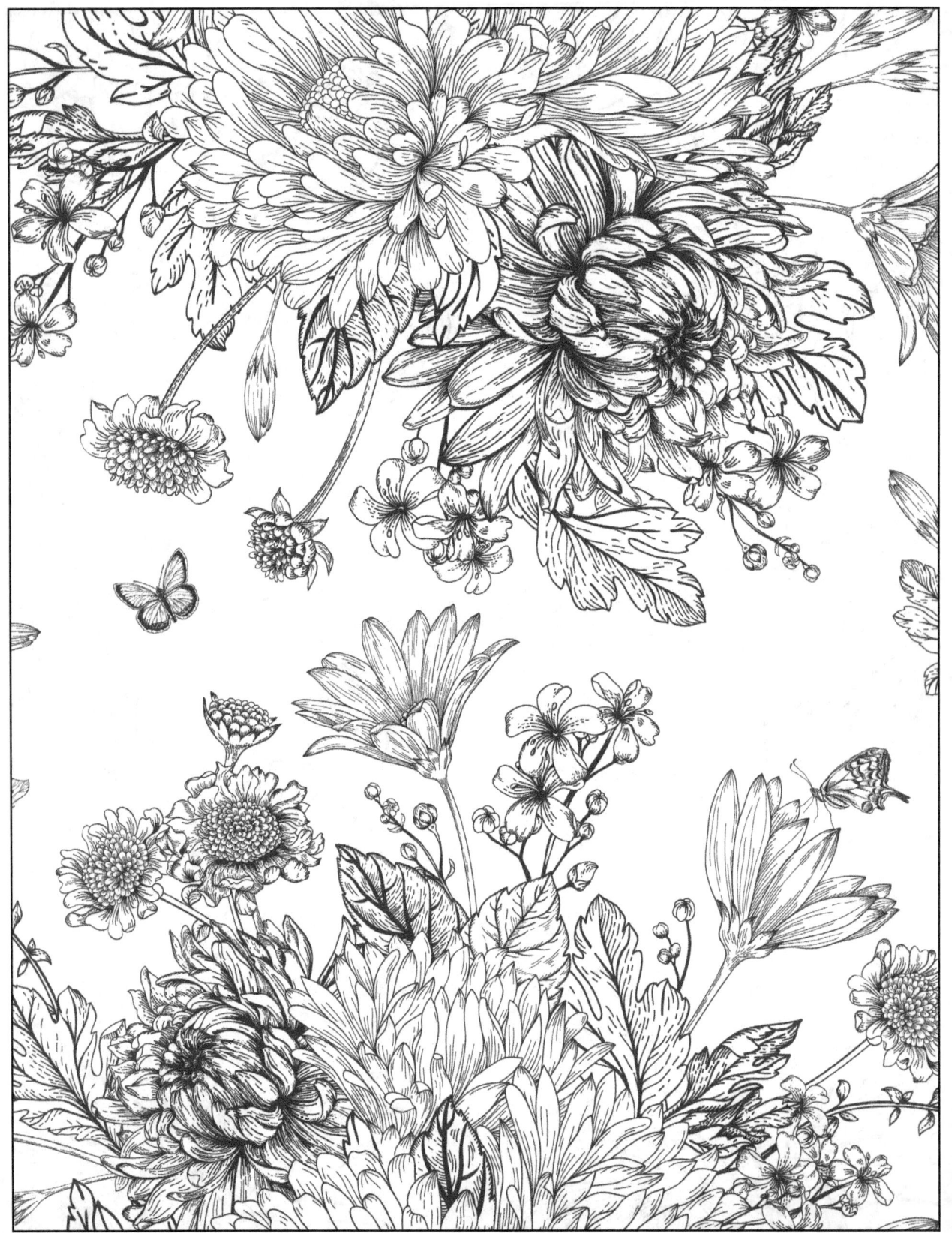

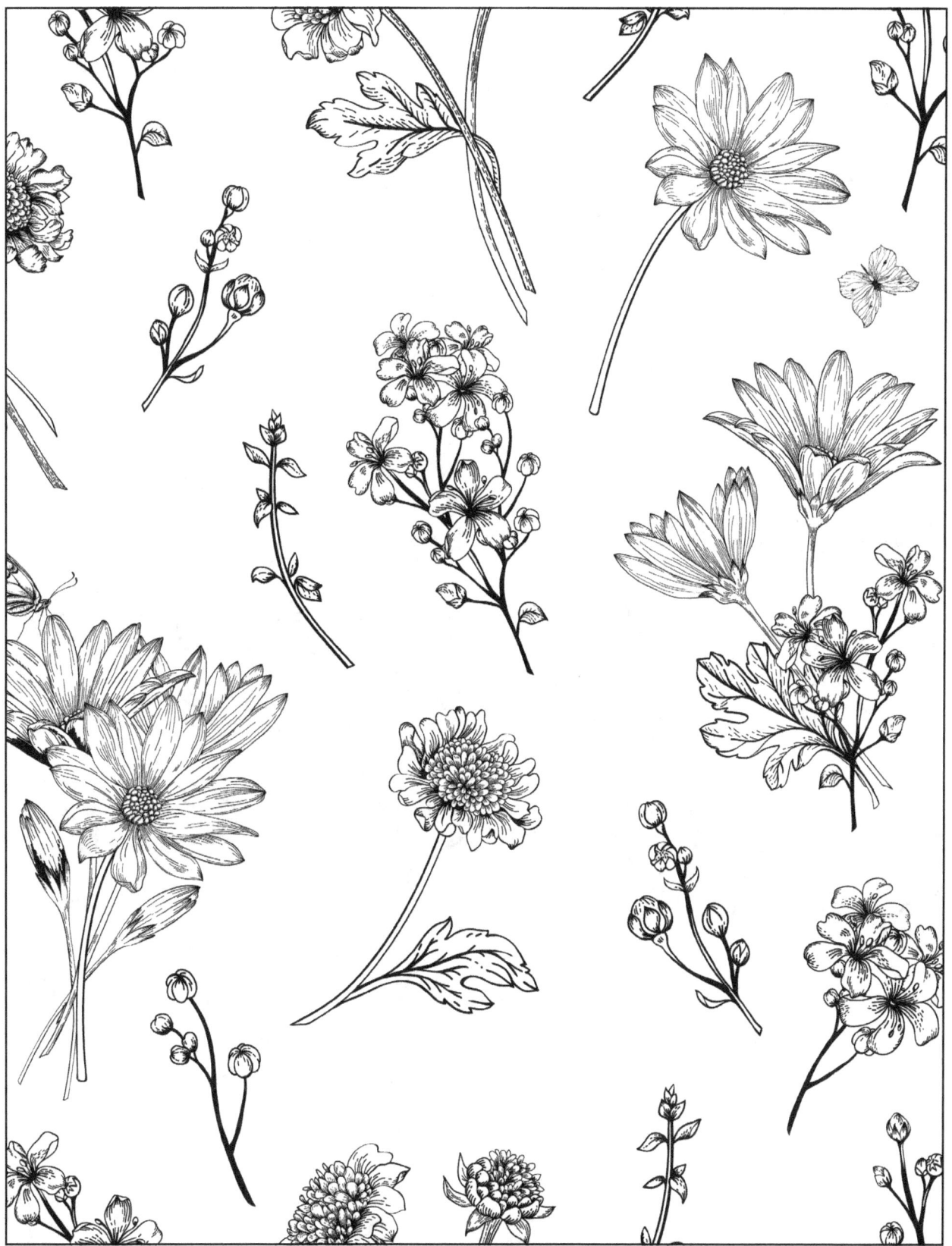

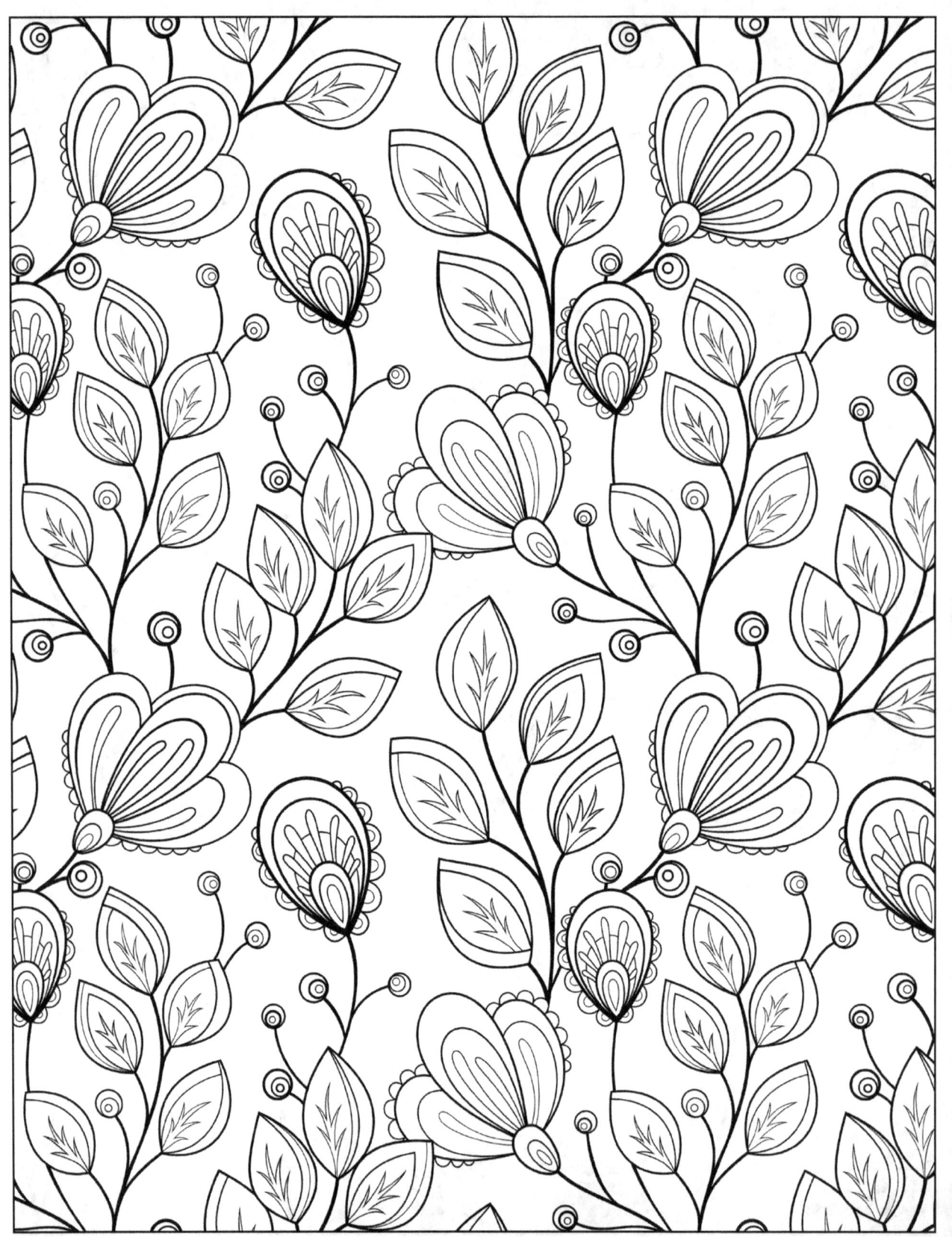

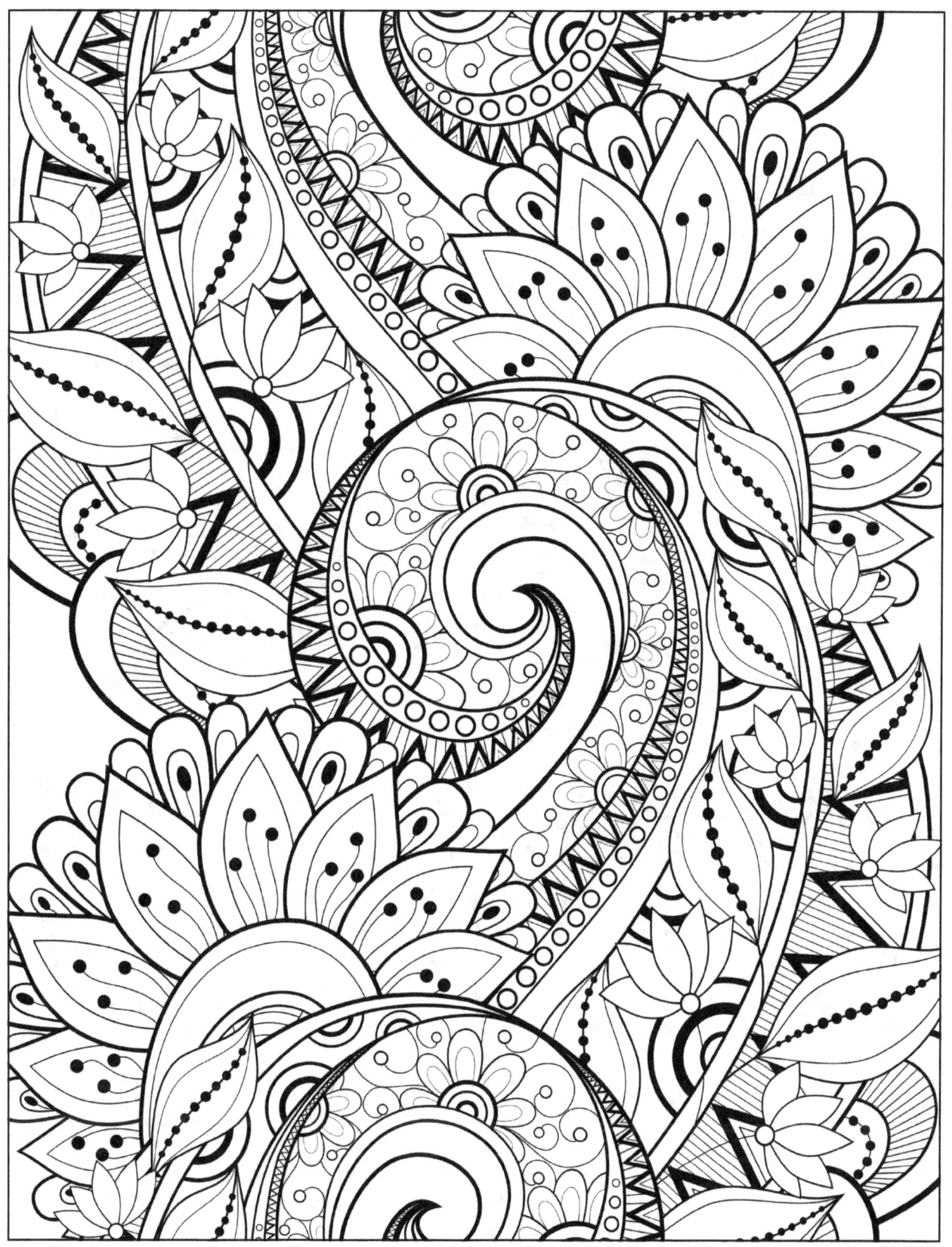

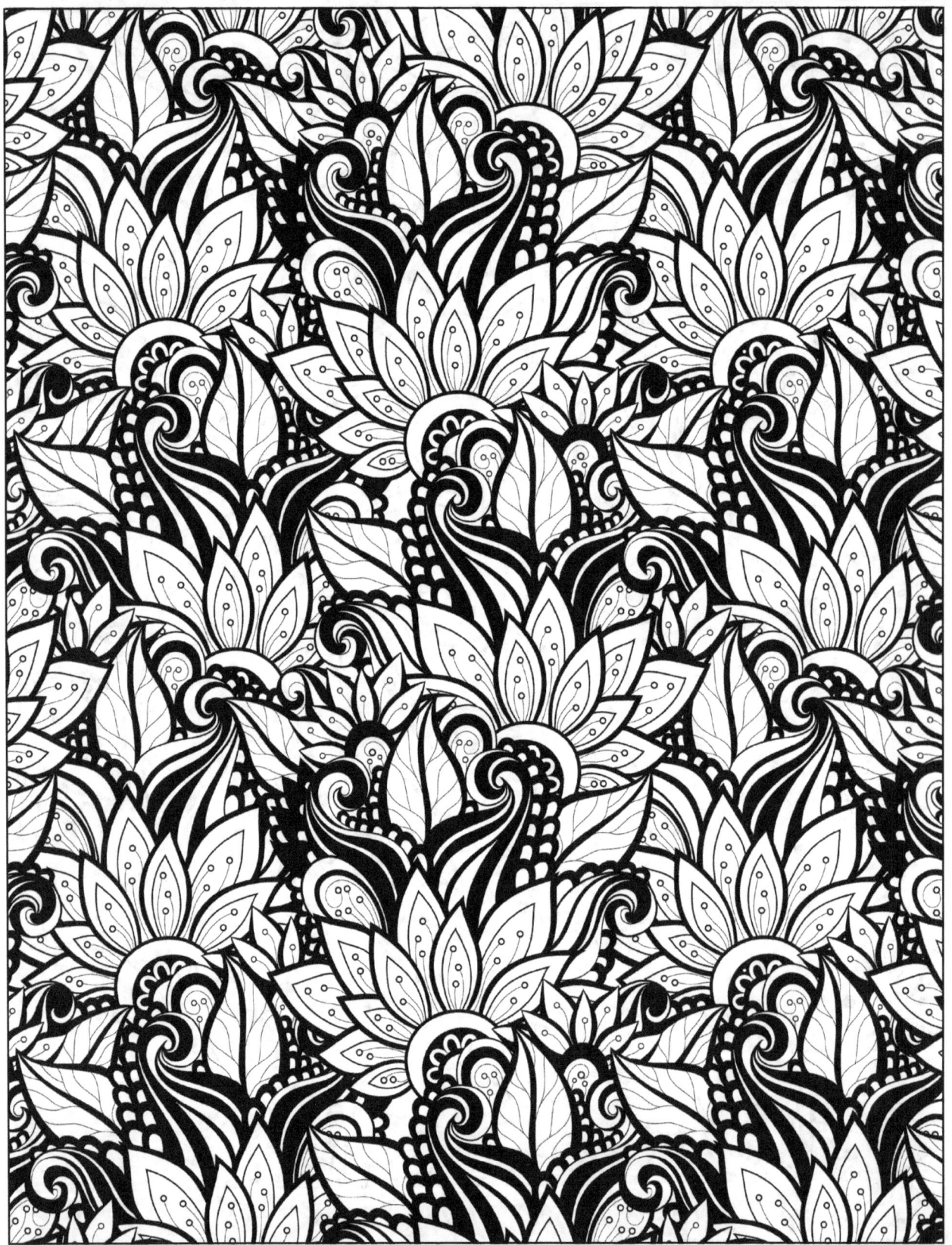

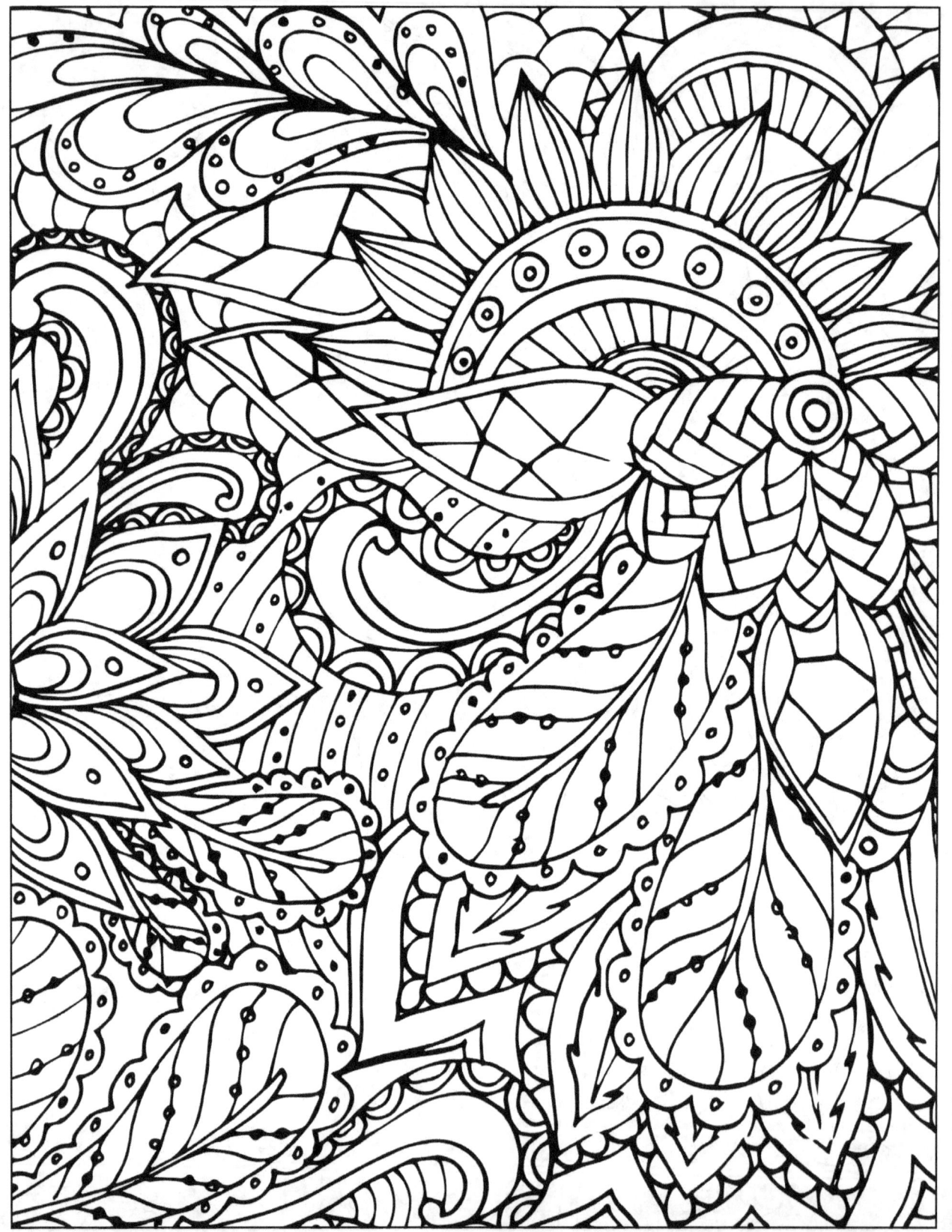

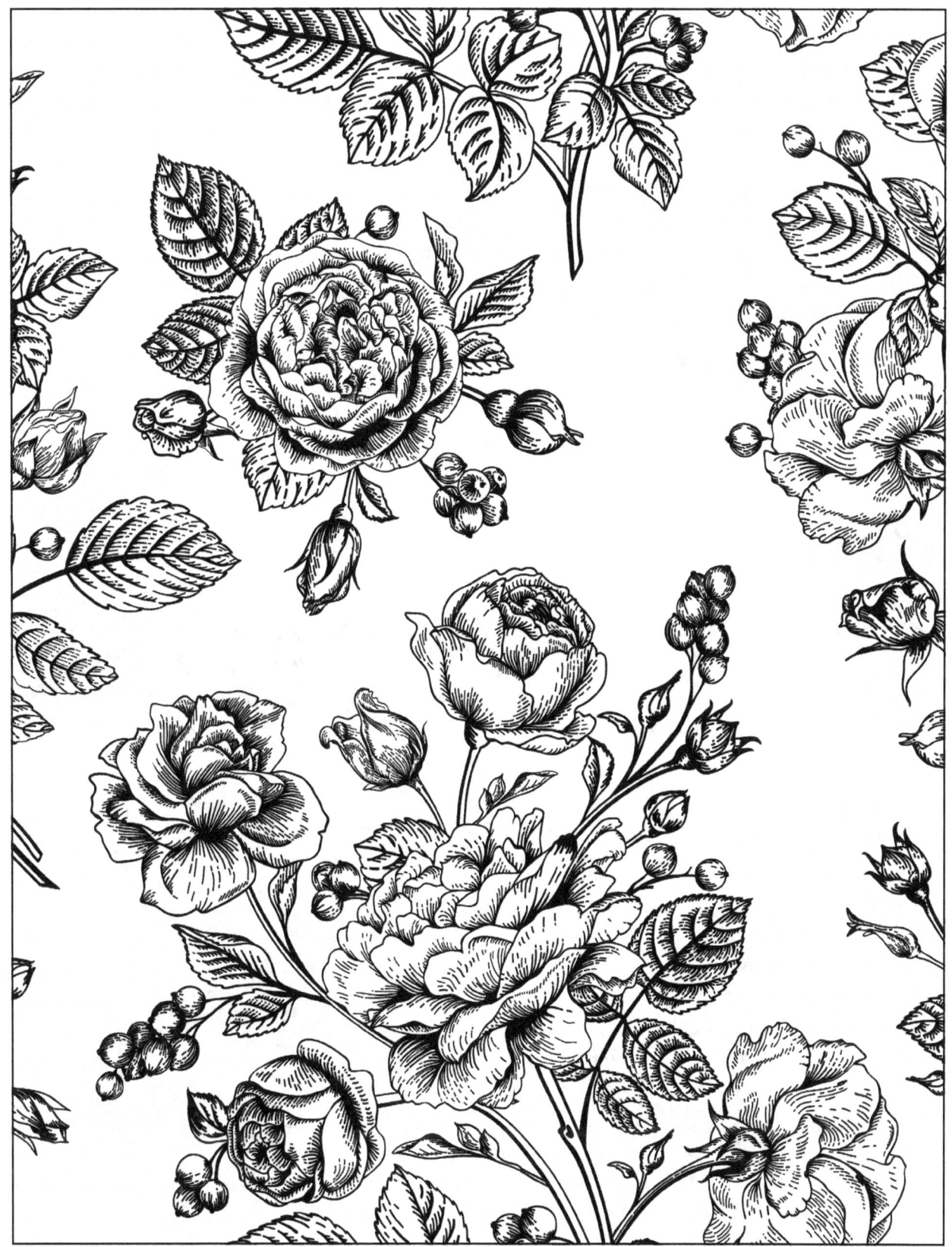

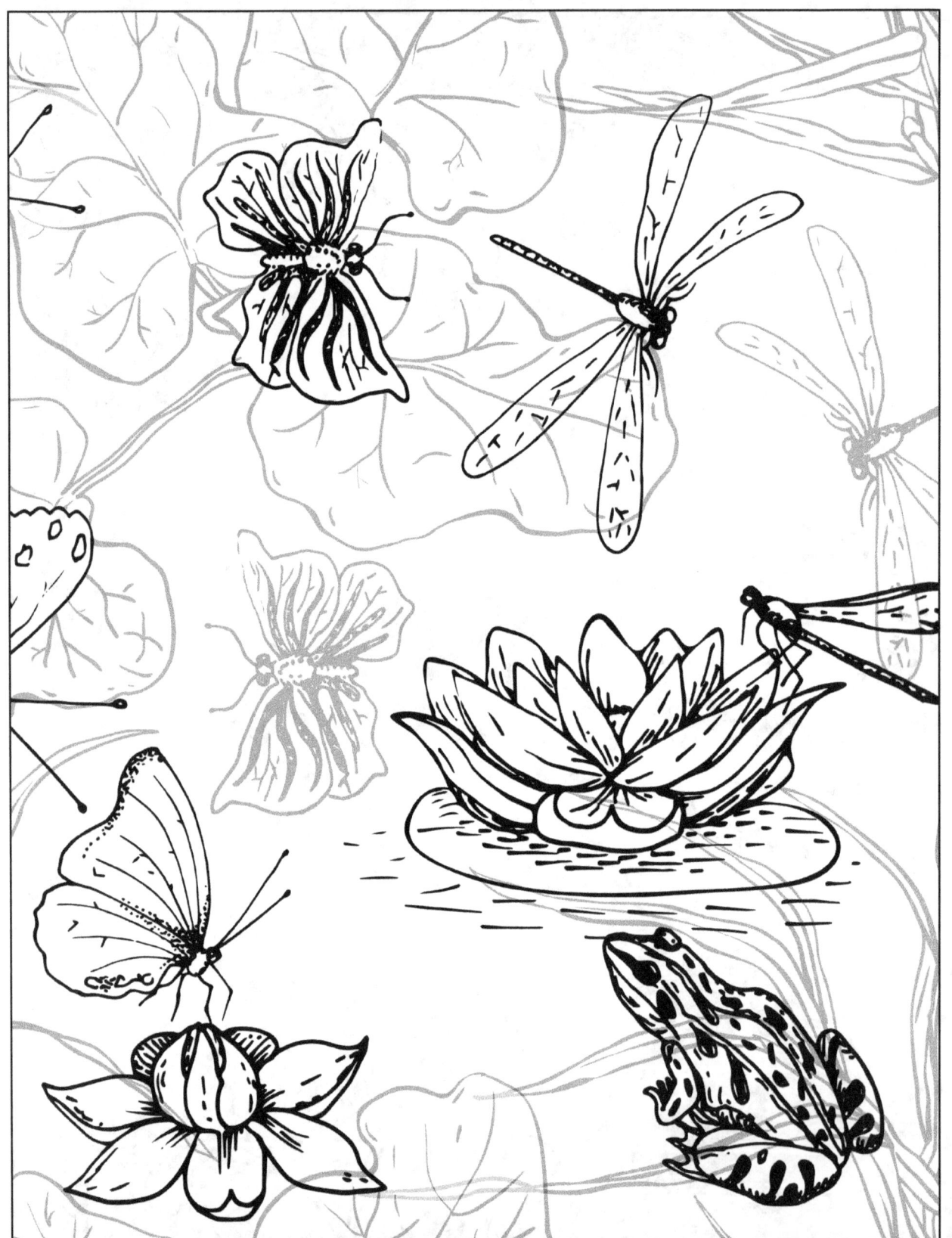

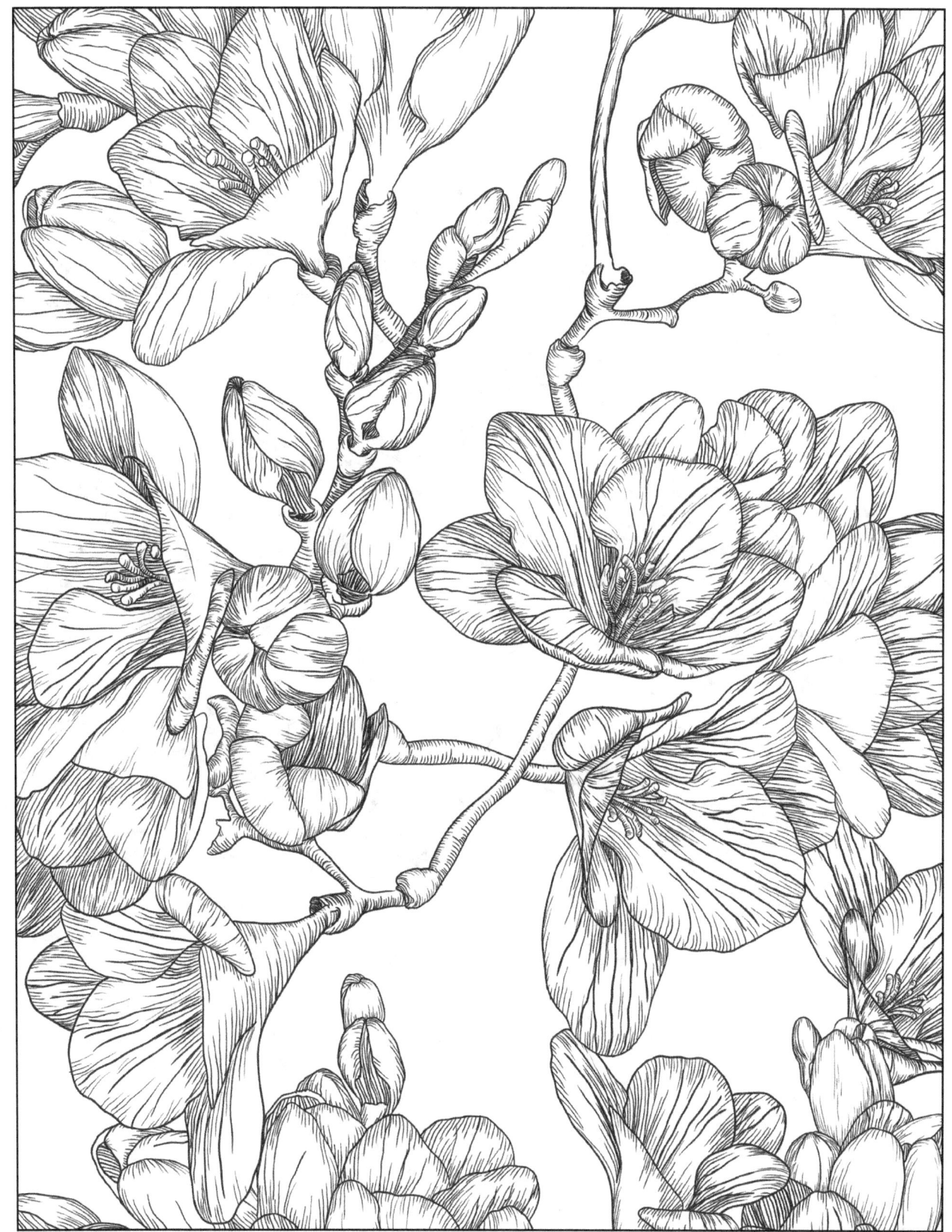

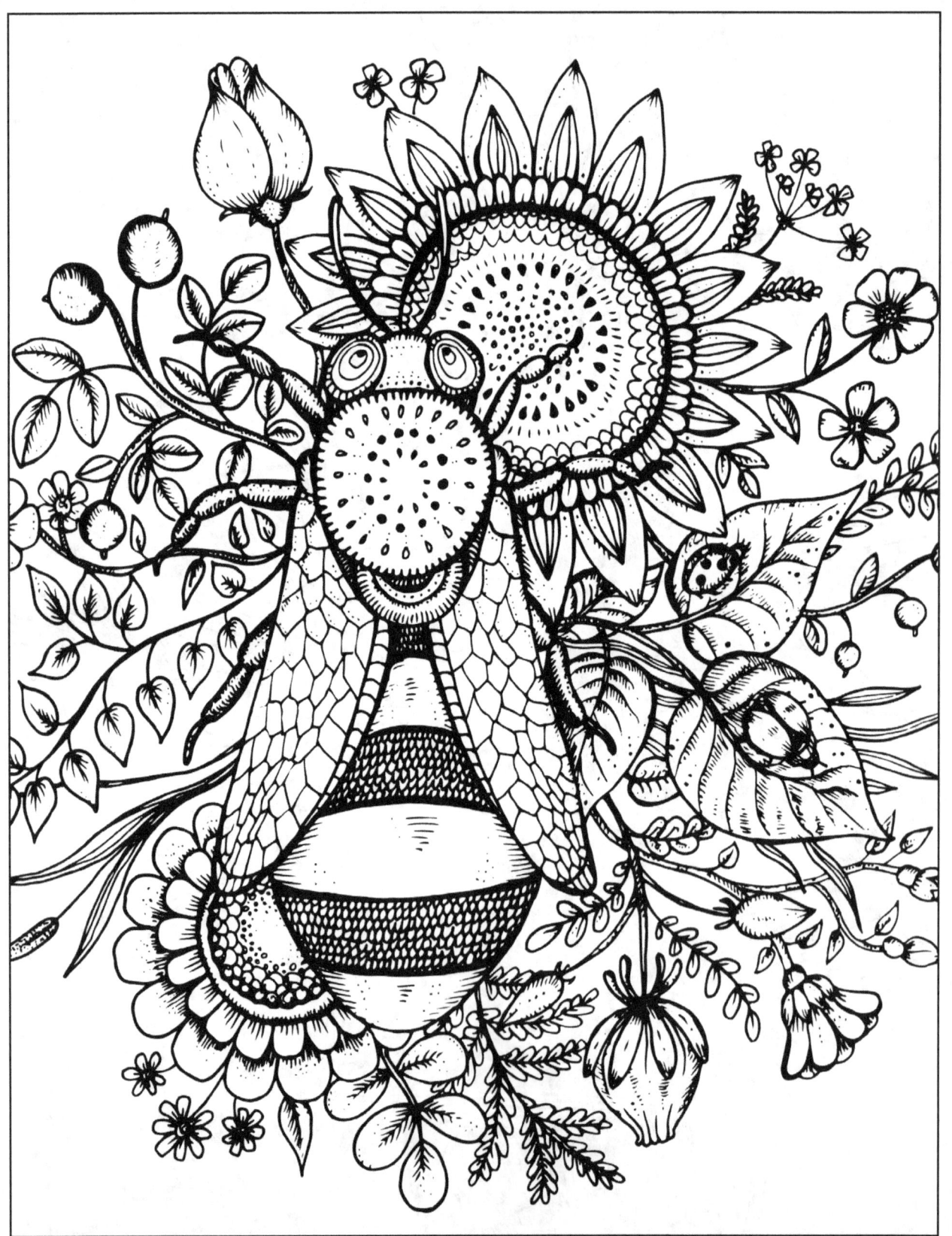

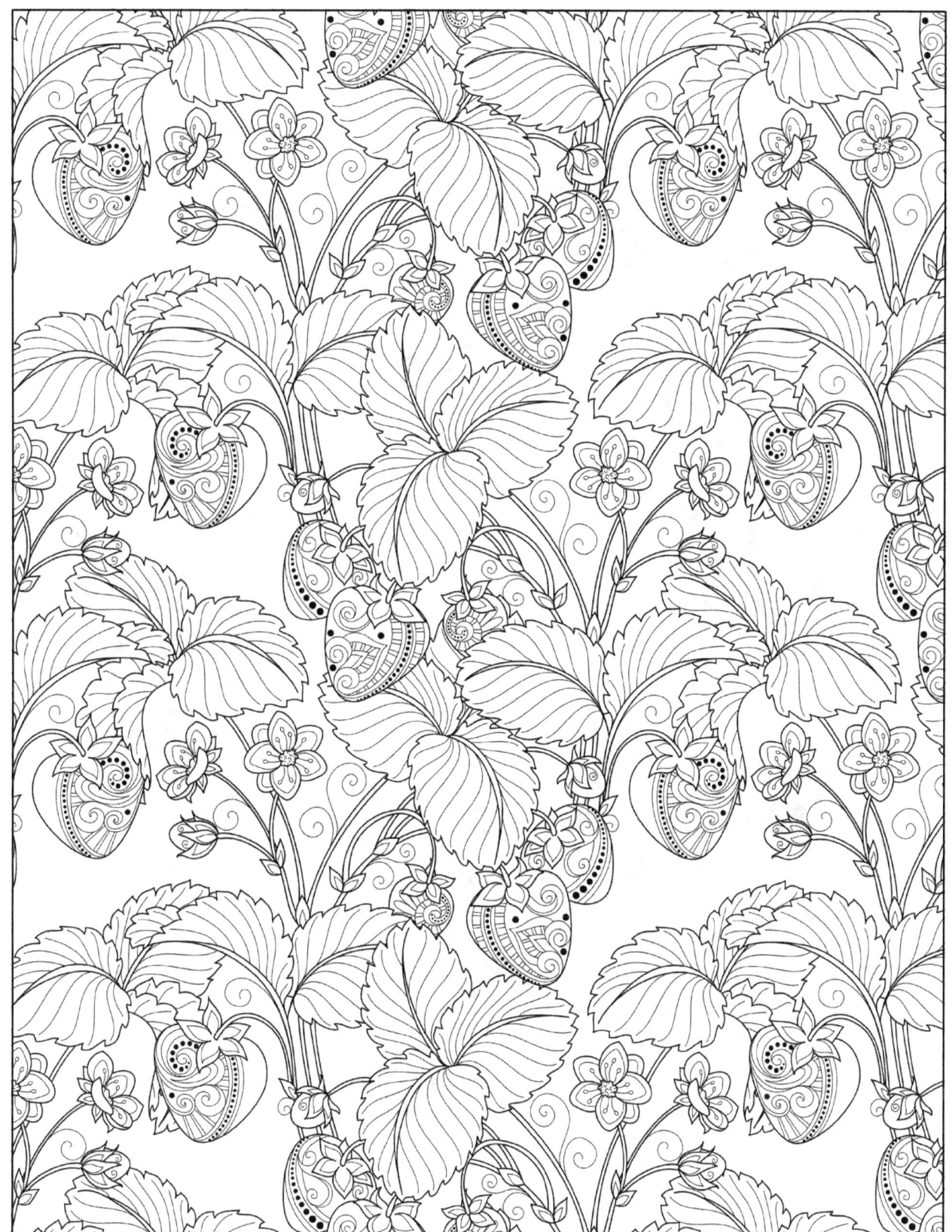

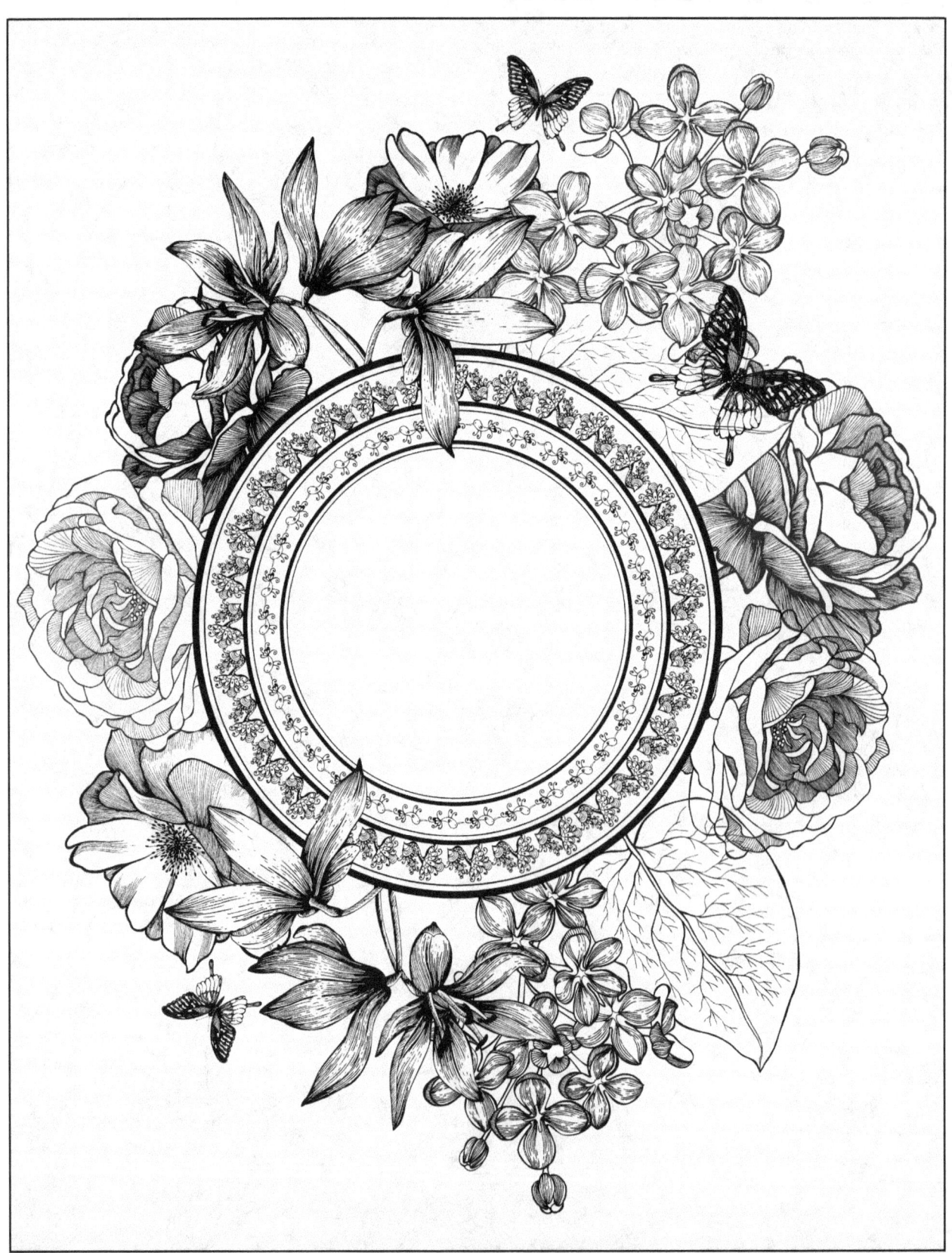

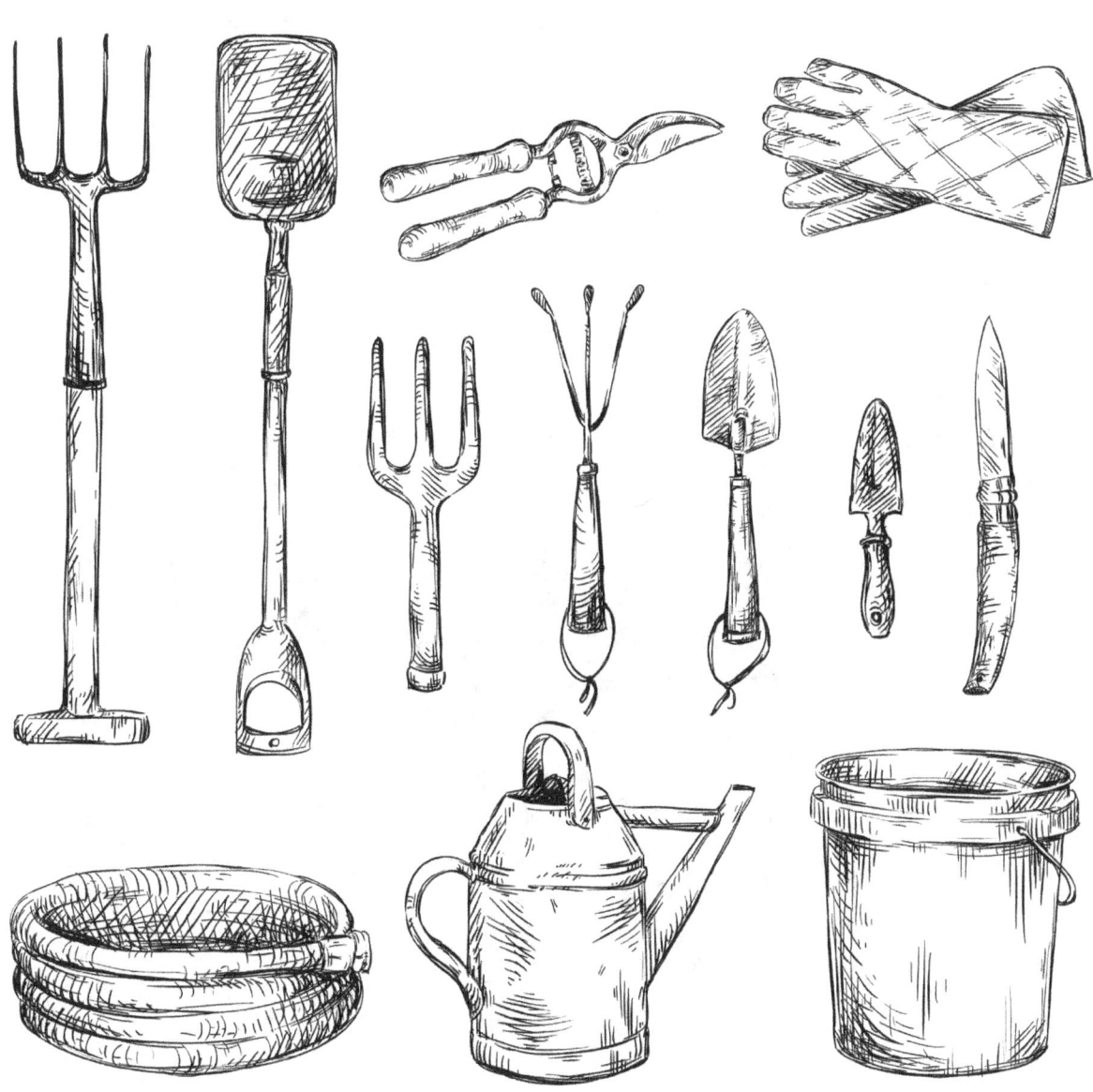

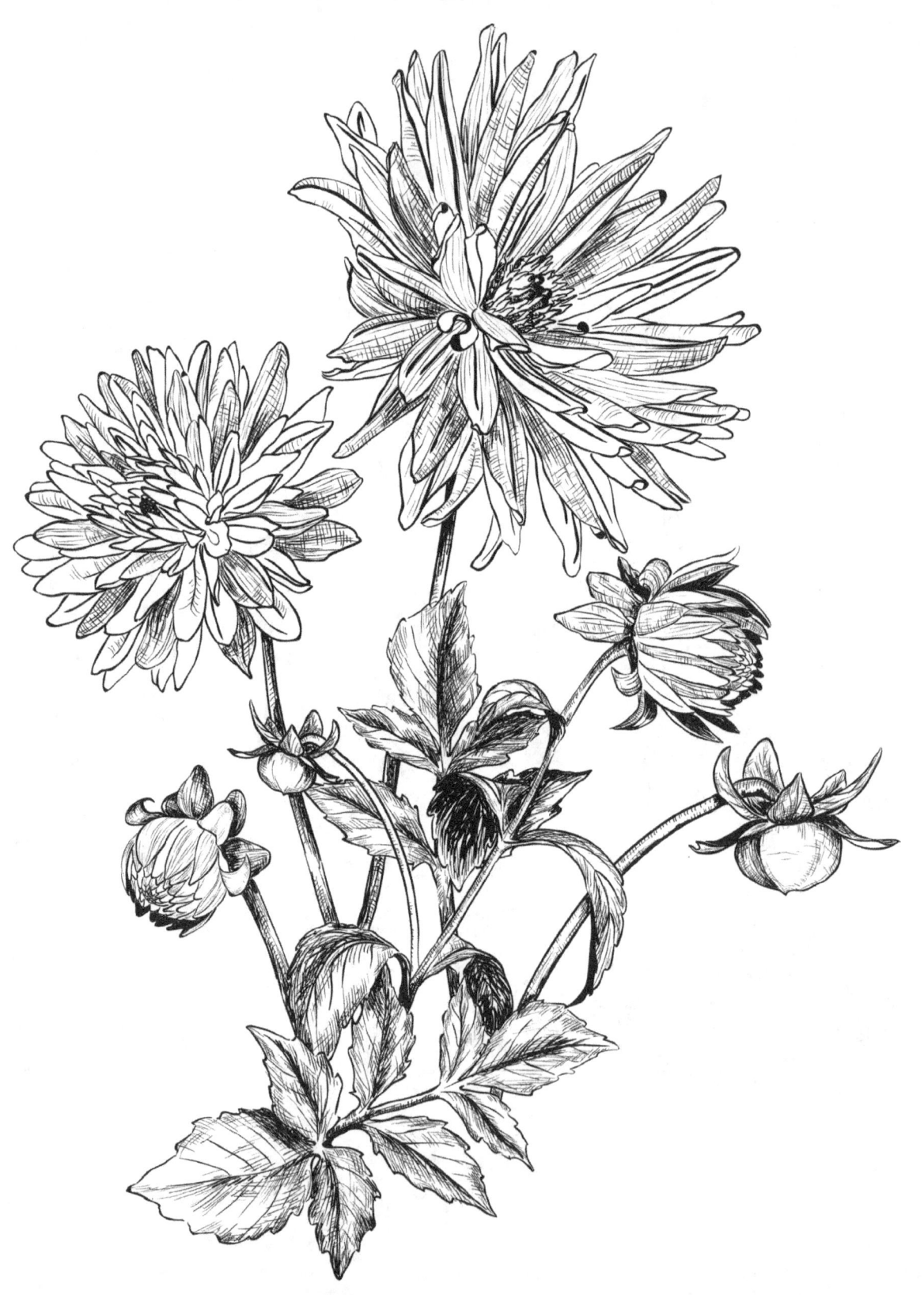

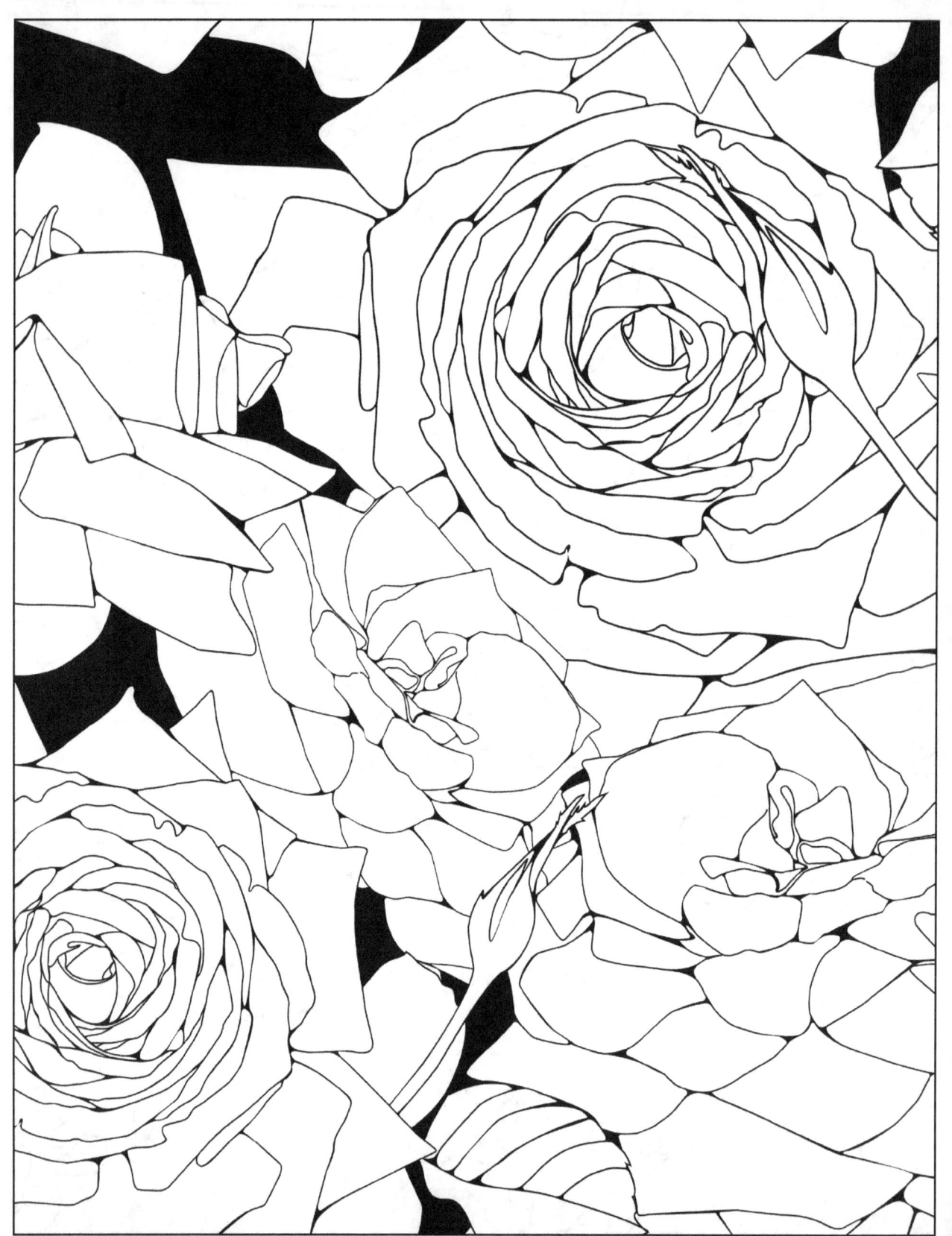

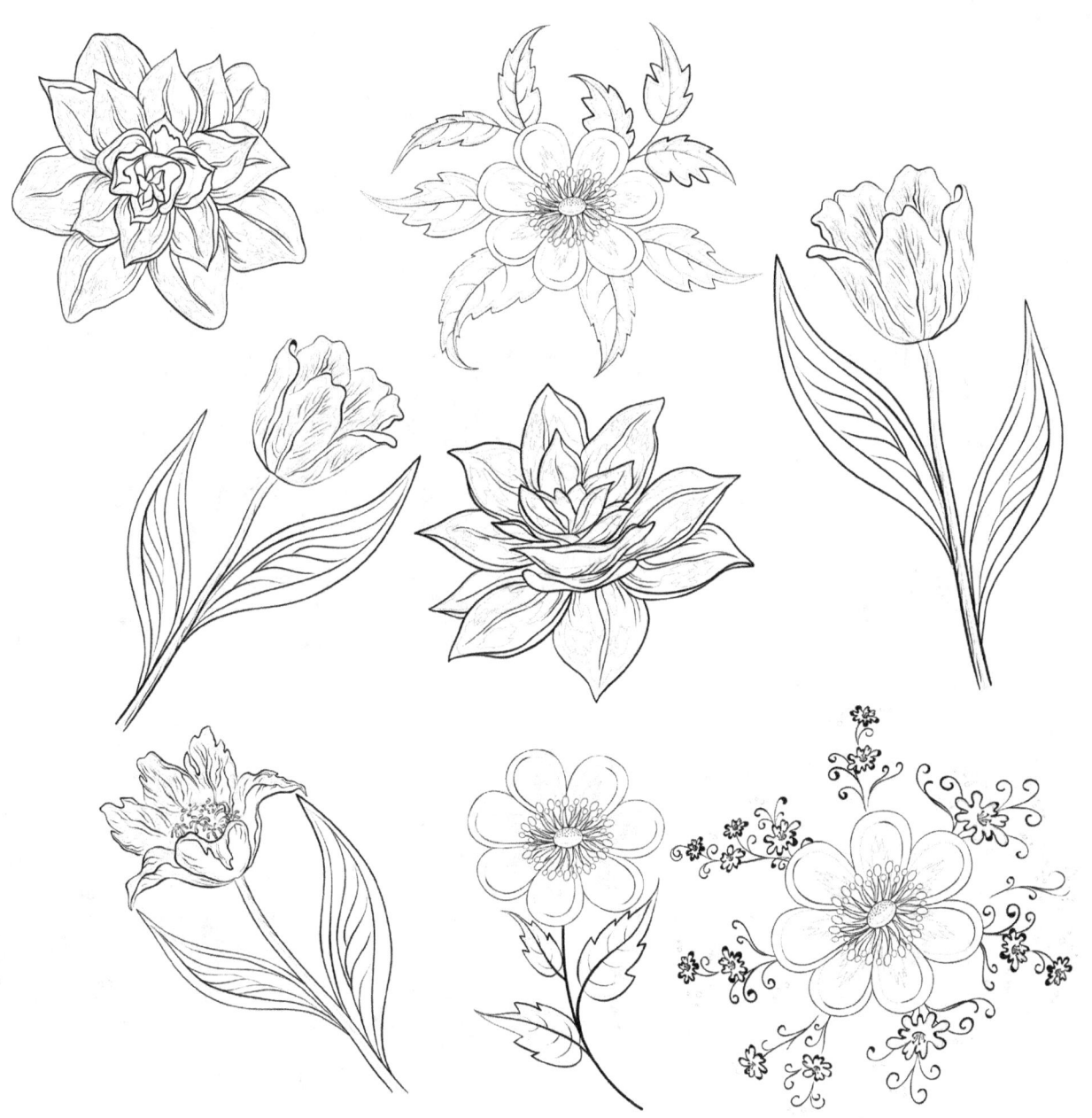

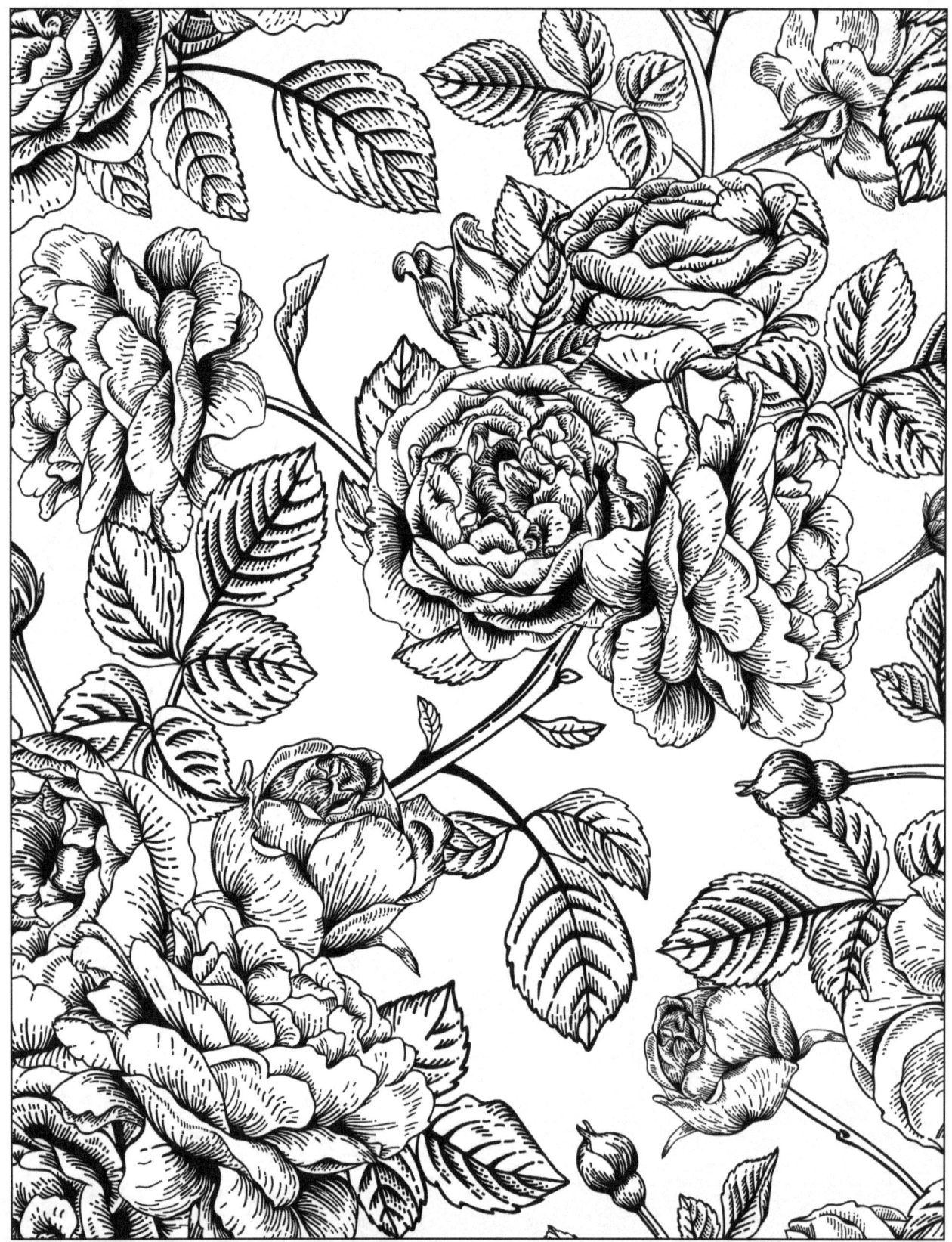

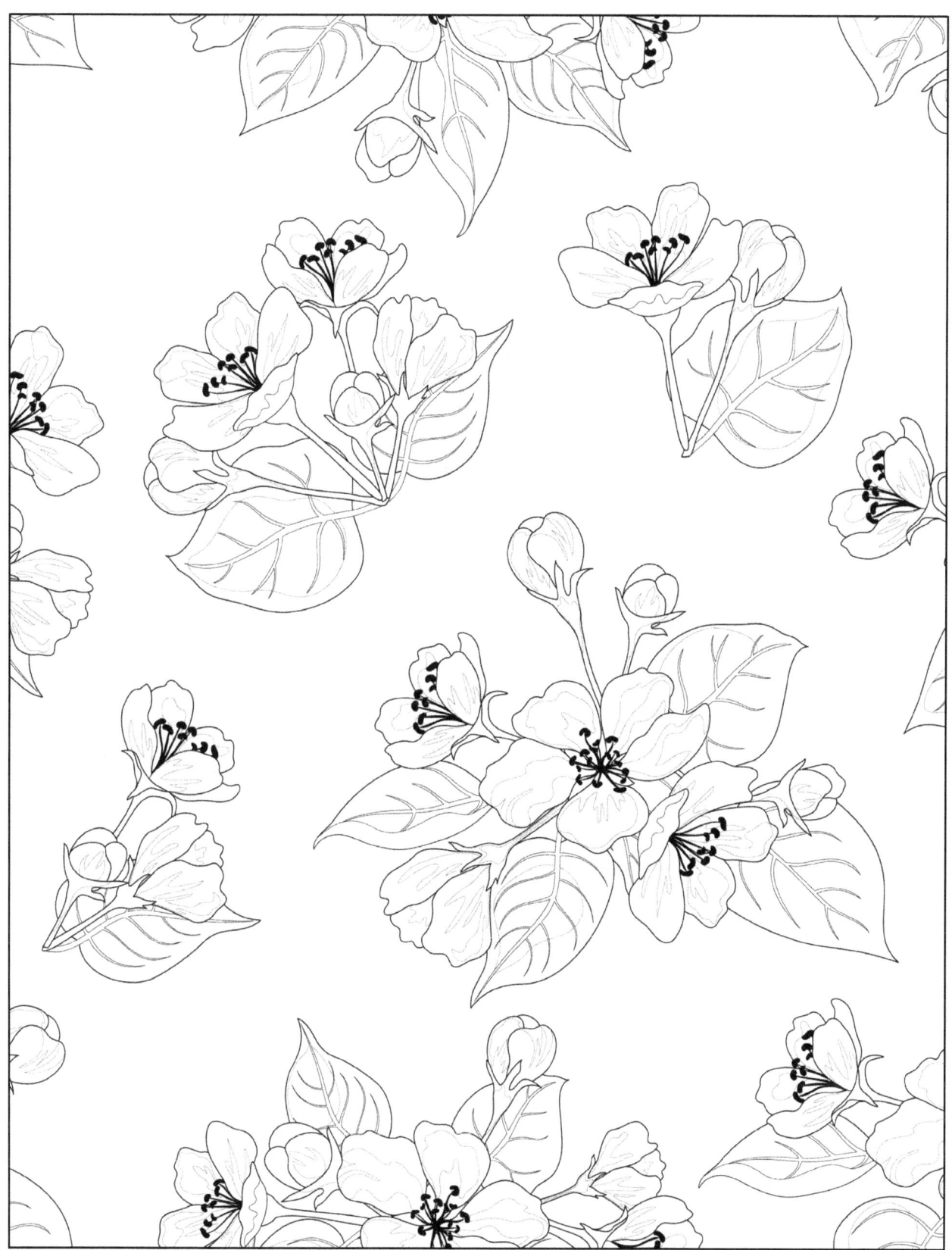

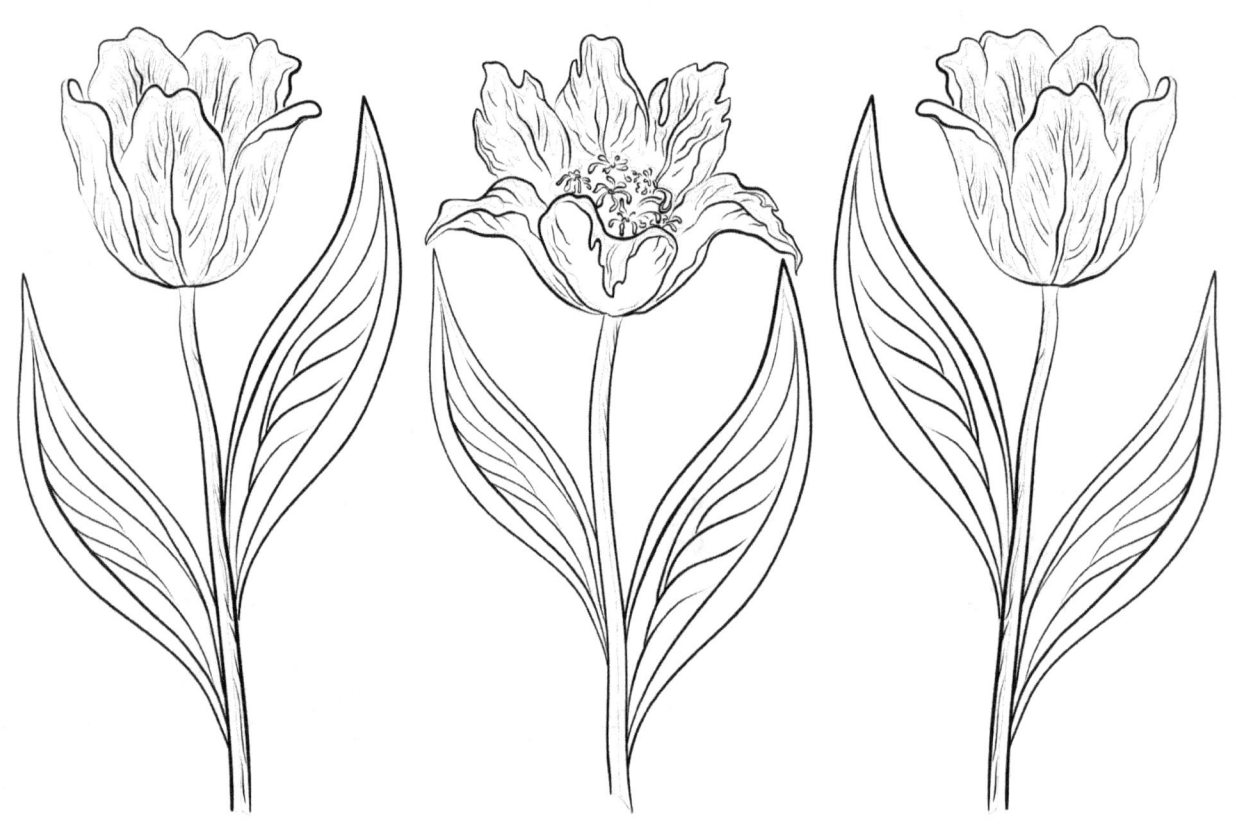

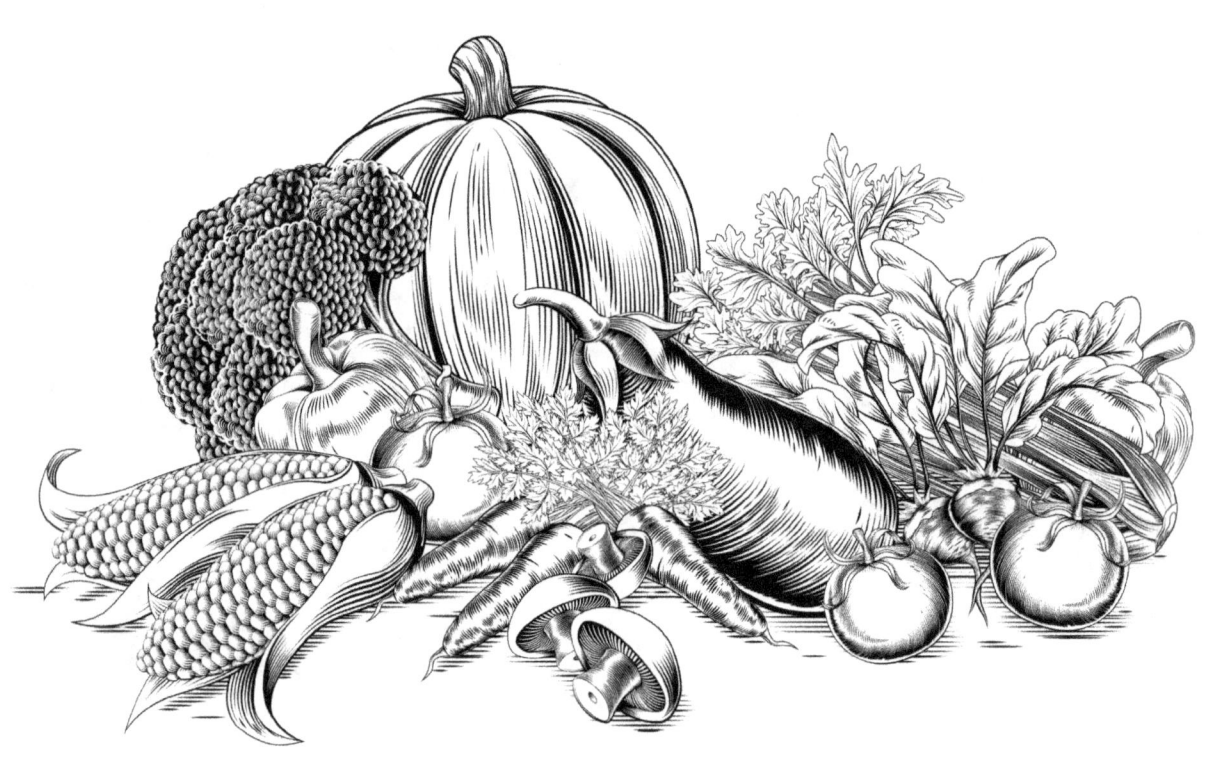

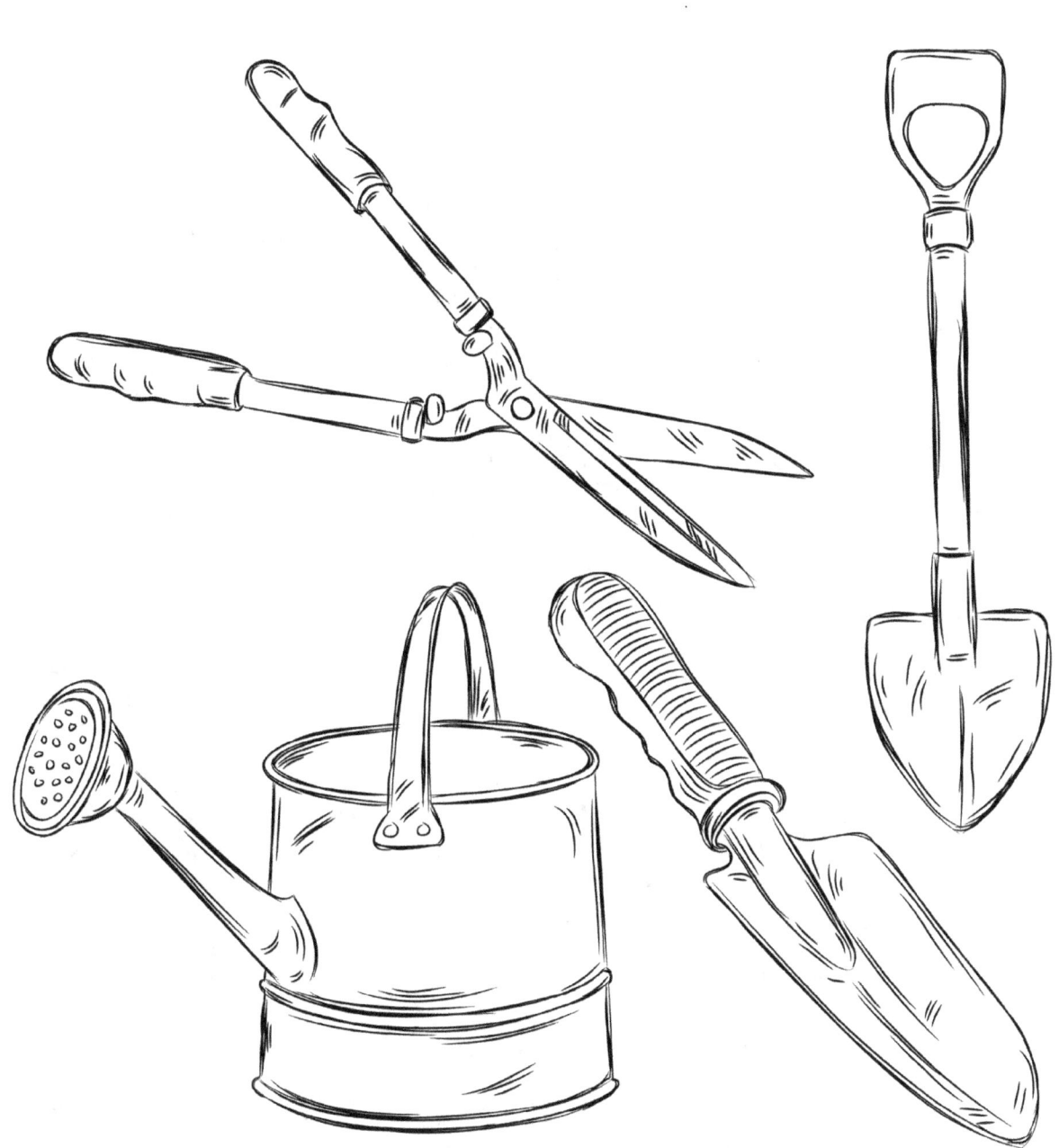

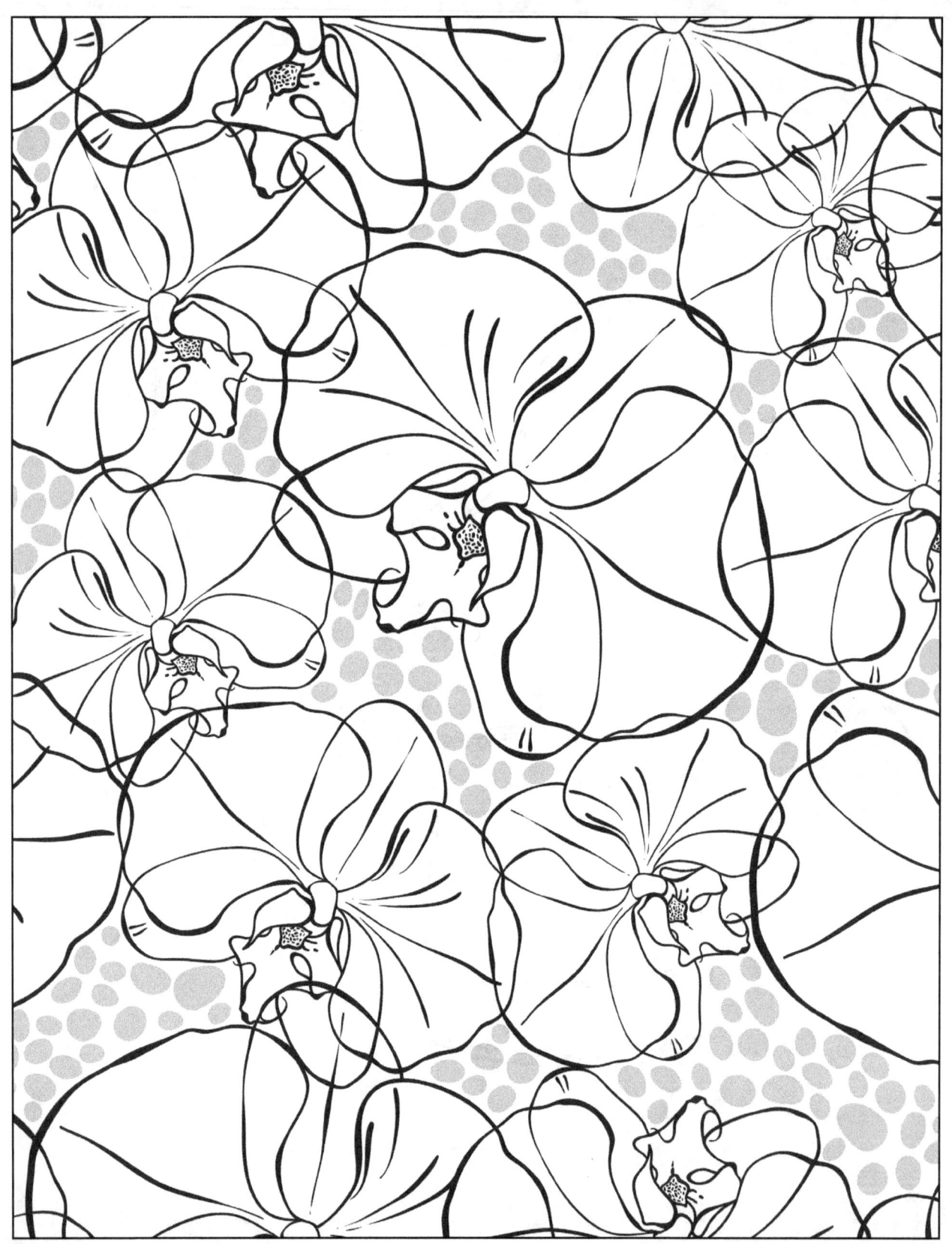

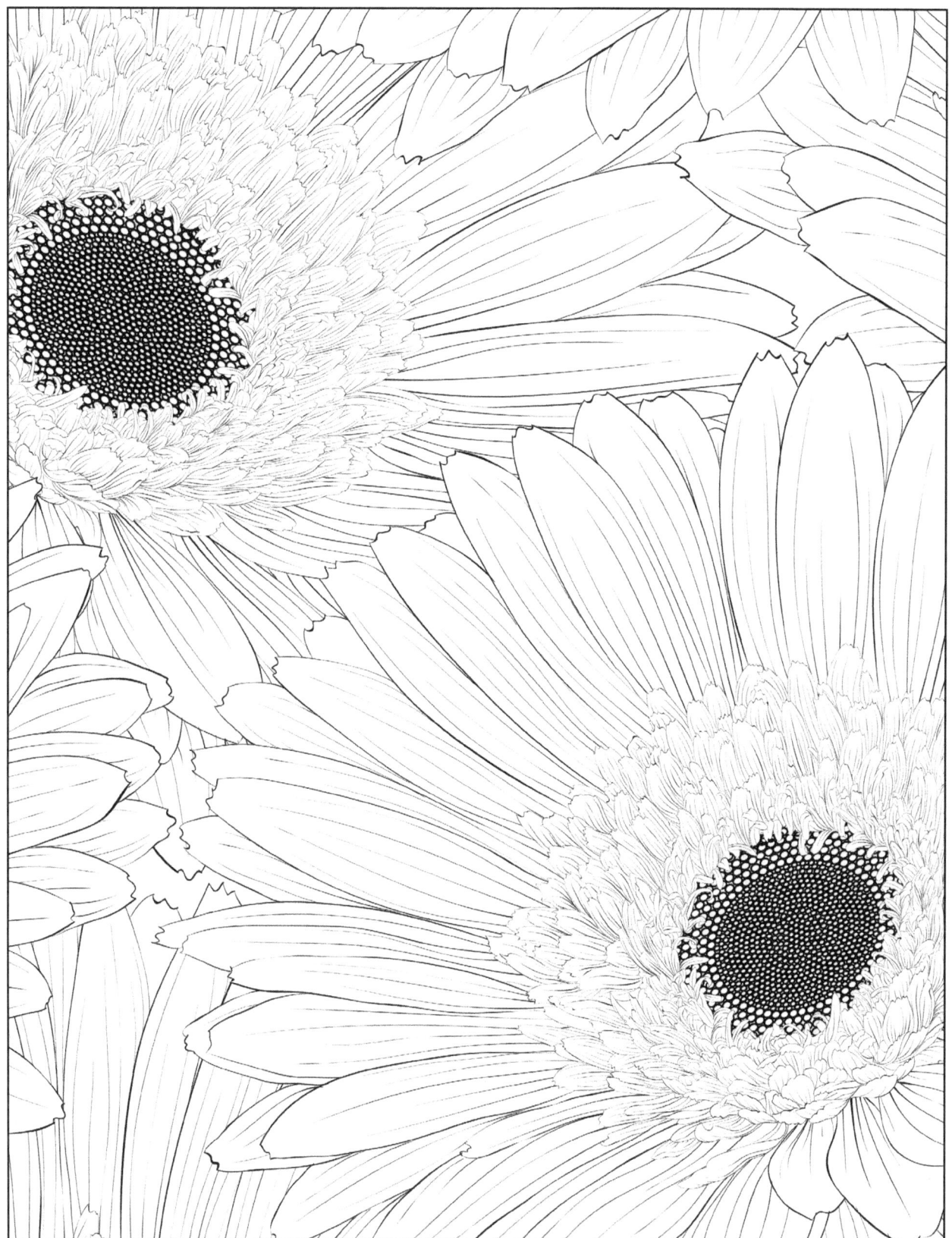

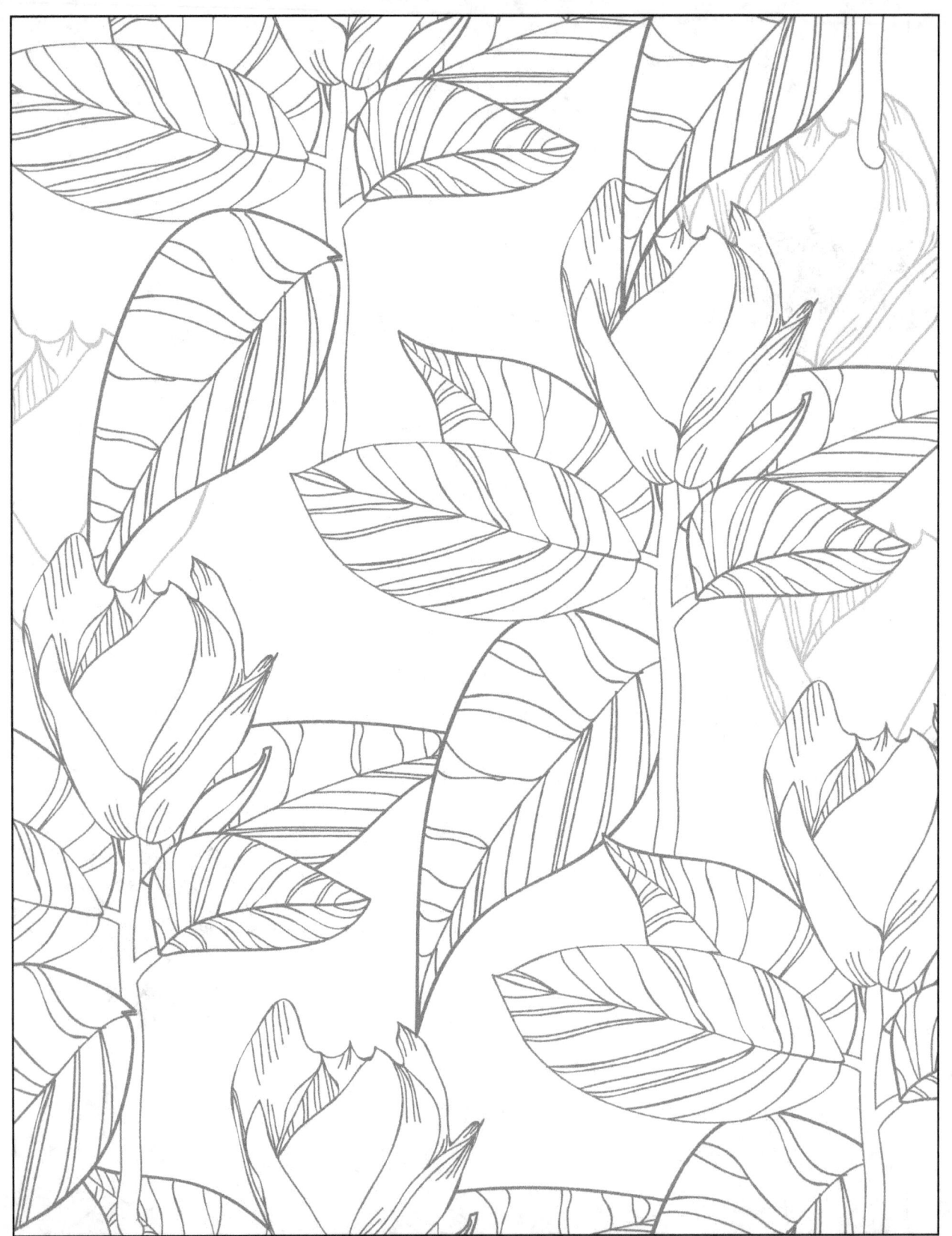

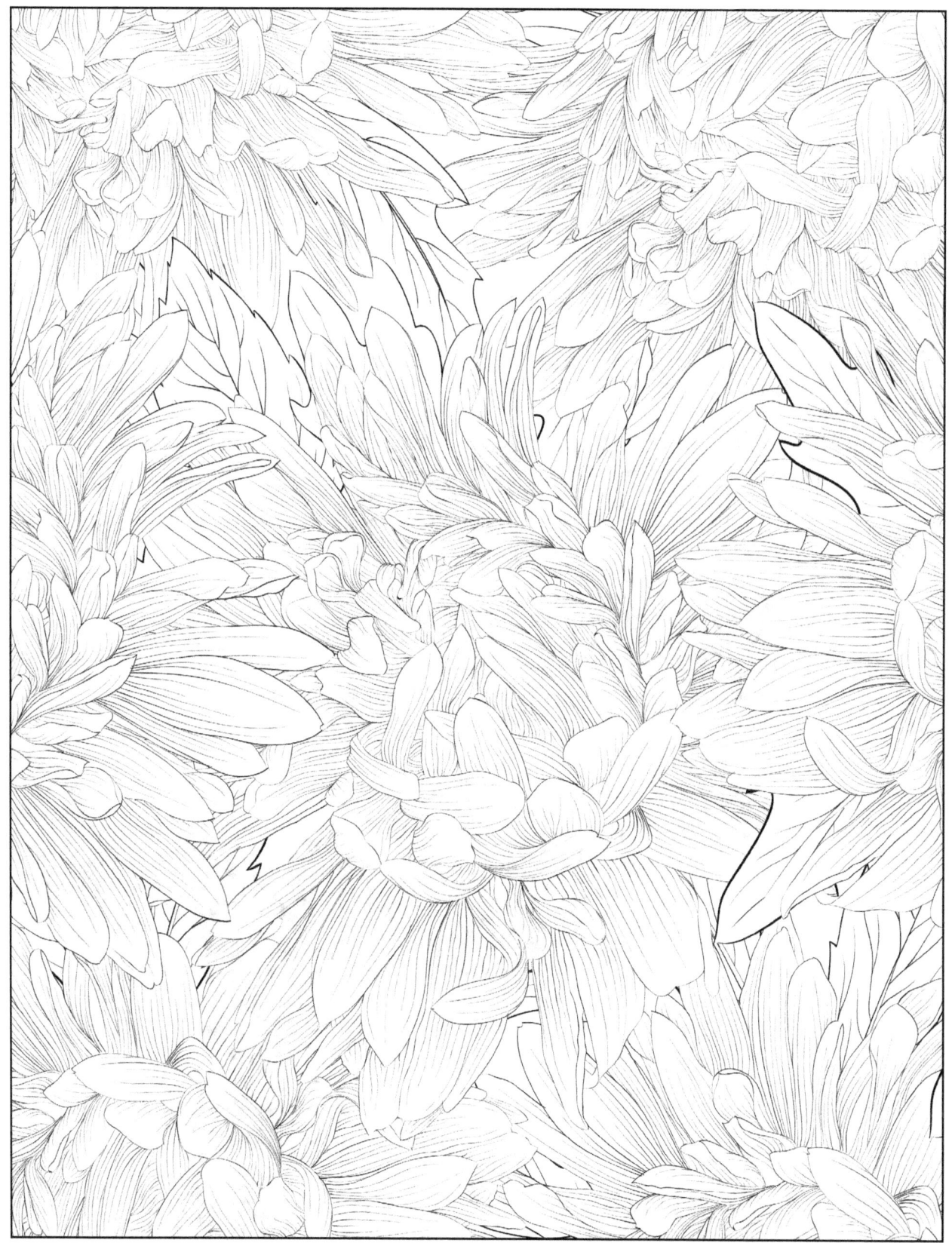

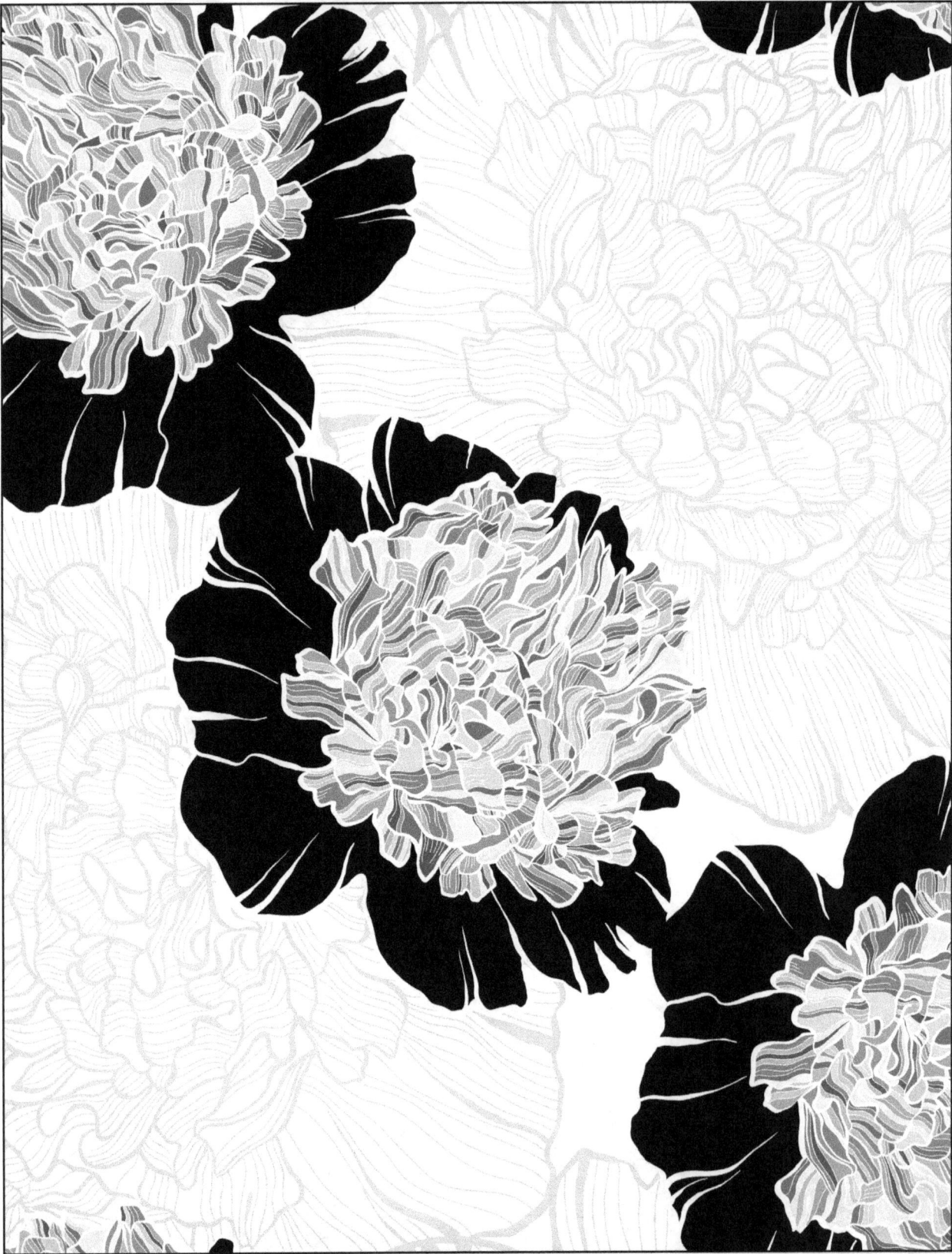

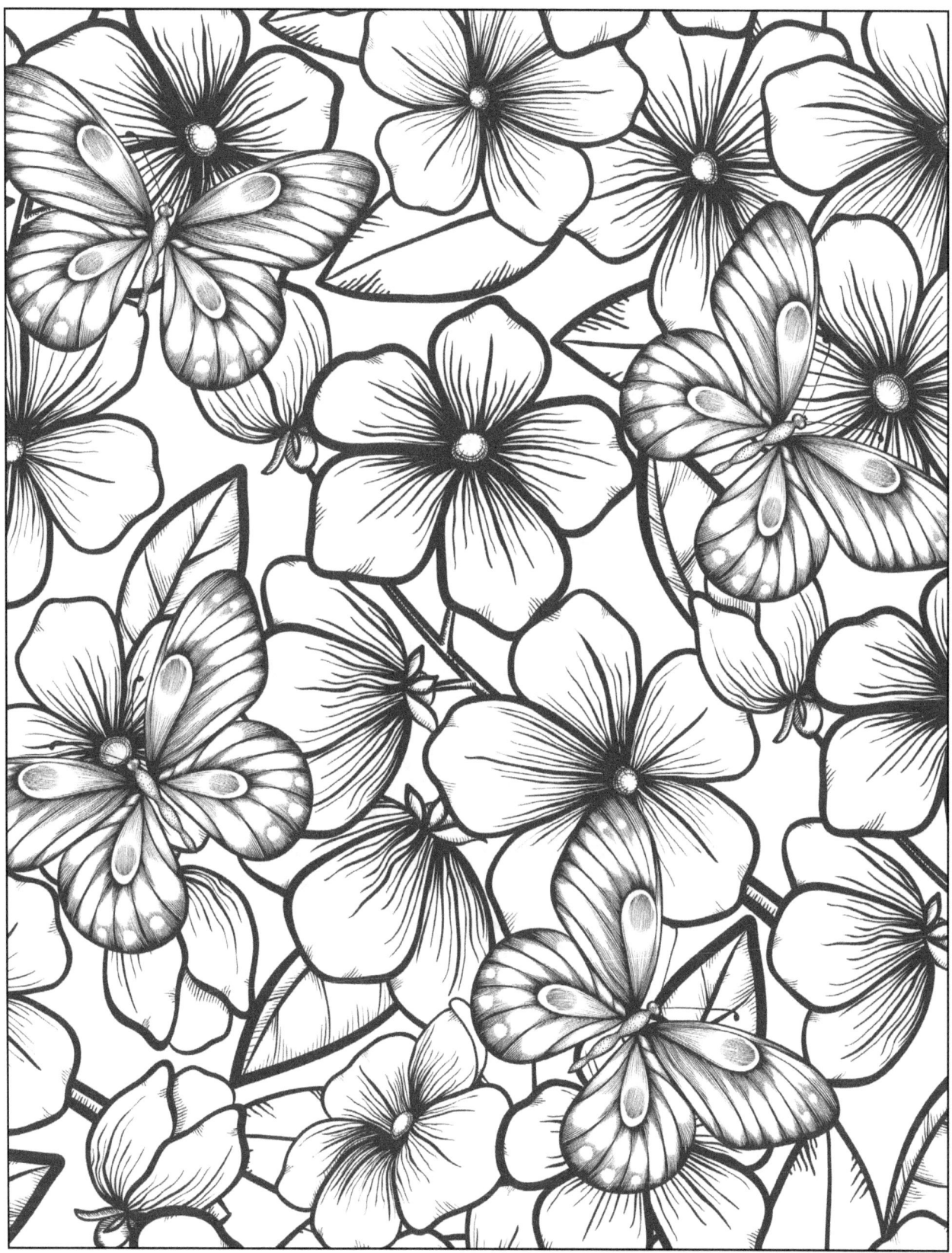